TRADITIONAL ENGLISH GRAMMAR

by

E. Darrell Holley, Ph.D.

Published by Randall House
114 Bush Road
Nashville, TN 37217

All Scripture quotations are taken from The Holy Bible, King James Version.

Printed in the United States of America

10-ISBN 0892655828
13-ISBN 9780892655823

Table of Contents

Chapter 1

A History of Traditional Grammar

The English adjective *traditional* is derived from the Latin verb *tradere*, "to hand over" or "to pass down." In trade, goods are handed over for money or other valuables. Tradition is the handing down of beliefs or customs or practices from generation to generation. The term *traditional grammar* as used in this book refers to the method of explaining language which has been used in the West and Near East since Classical times. There are, of course, other methods of explaining language. As will be seen later, there are those—especially in the twentieth century—who have rejected the tradition completely and the philosophical premises on which it is based. However, traditional grammar has a long and venerable history in the intellectual life of Western culture.

The Greeks

The study of grammar originated, evidently, among the Greeks. The *grammatikoi* ("grammarians") were the teachers of Greek. Students first learned the letters (*grammata*) of the Greek alphabet. Next they proceeded to simple syllables, then words. The *grammatikos* taught his students to read by using Homer's *Iliad* and *Odyssey*. As a student progressed, he took up a thorough study of Greek literature, which necessarily required an understanding of Greek grammar. Grammar was, from its origin, intimately connected with literary studies: one learned grammar in order to understand the meaning of the text, and one learned grammar by parsing or analyzing passages from the text.

Various Greek authors allude to the study of grammar. Though there are relatively few works which have survived from the earliest times of ancient Greece, there are several references to grammatical education. The historian Herodotus tells how (about 494 BC) over a hundred boys were killed on the island of Chios when the roof of their school collapsed while they were "learning their letters."[1] Plato refers to grammar, and, especially in his dialogue called the "Cratylus," he raises questions related to grammar or the study of words. Aristotle also refers to the *grammatikoi* and grammar. In his *Poetics* he discusses the eight basic parts of speech.

---

[1] Herodotus, *The History*, David Grene, trans. (Chicago: University of Chicago, 1987), 6.27.

The earliest grammar book in existence is the *Tekhne Grammatike* ("The Grammatical Art") written by Dionysius Thrax about 100 BC. Dionysius Thrax (ca. 170-ca. 90 BC) was perhaps a Thracian ("Thrax") or a descendant of emigrants from Thrace (a region north of Greece). Perhaps for him Greek was a "second language," as it would be termed today. For whatever reasons, Dionysius pursued a literary education. He studied under Aristarchus, the head of the famous library in Alexandria, in Egypt. The scholars at Alexandria (really more of an ancient college than a modern library) were interested in Greek grammar as a preparation for the study of Greek literature. Later, Dionysius taught Greek grammar on the island of Rhodes.

At some point in his scholarly career, Dionysius Thrax authored his book on grammar. A small work (only about a dozen pages long), the *Tekhne Grammatike* is nonetheless extremely important in the history of grammar. It had a lasting influence on the Western grammatical tradition for the next two thousand years. Even its name is interesting. Its topic is a *tekhne* (related to our words *technique* and *technical*), a skill or art, specifically the *grammatike tekhne*, the "grammatical art." Its title comes ultimately from *gramma*, the Greek word meaning "a letter of the alphabet." In the plural it came to mean "literature," much like the English word *letters*.

Though the work is primarily concerned with literary criticism, it includes a brief but thorough discussion of the parts of speech. The first ten chapters (actually, each is only about a paragraph in length) deal with phonics, and the last ten focus on the *logos* ("thought" or "sentence"). Included is a presentation of eight parts of speech: the noun, verb, participle, article, pronoun, preposition, adverb, and conjunction. (Notice that Dionysius lists participles separately from verbs and lists articles as a separate part of speech. He includes adjectives as a subset of nouns and interjections as a type of adverb.)

The importance of this little book cannot be overstated. For hundreds of years it was used as a guide to an understanding of the grammar of Greek, then Latin, then English (and French and Spanish and all the modern languages). Indeed, it was used even by such diverse peoples as Arabs, Armenians, and Syrians. It is, in effect, the proto-grammar book of the West. Interestingly, it does not deal with the question of the importance of grammar; it is assumed *a priori* that grammar is an important and necessary function of readers and writers.[2] This concept of the innate nature of grammar expressed by Dionysius Thrax was not seriously questioned until the latter half of the nineteenth century AD.

---

[2] The term *a priori* is Latin for "from the earlier" or "from the prior." *A priori* concepts are fundamental assumptions recognized as truth.

The Romans

No doubt there were other ancient Greeks who wrote on grammar and related topics, but their works have not survived. That the *Tekhne* of Dionysius Thrax did survive is due to its continuing importance in Greek and then Roman education. Later, as the Romans conquered more and more of the Mediterranean world, their own language and their own literature (much of it based on Greek models) became more and more important. People in the far-flung provinces of the Empire (which stretched from Mesopotamia to Britannia, from Germany to Palestine to North Africa) needed to understand Latin.

In a famous line from his *Epistles*, the Roman poet Horace says: "Graecia capta ferum victorem cepit et artes intulit agresti Latio." ("Greece, having been captured, captured her fierce conqueror and brought the arts to rustic Latium.")[3] The Romans first confronted Hellenic culture as it was represented by the Greek settlers in Magna Graecia, the ancient Greek colony in southern Italy. Eventually, in the second century BC, they succeeded in dominating Greece itself. The Romans might have conquered Greece, but, as Horace noted, Greek culture, including its language and literature, soon conquered Rome. Greek became a part of the education of every aristocratic Roman male. If possible, a wealthy family might even purchase an educated Greek slave to serve as a *paidagoigos* or tutor for their sons. (One famous *paidagoigus* was Aesop, the supposed author of the *Fables*.) How Greek grammar and literature first arrived in Rome is debatable. According to one story, about 168 BC, Crates, from the city of Mallus in Asia Minor, came to Rome on a diplomatic mission. While there, however, he fell and broke his leg. During his convalescence in Rome he gave lectures, comparing and contrasting the Greek and Latin languages and their literatures.

The first to attempt a reformulation of Dionysius's work for a Roman audience was a certain Apollonius, who lived in the second century BC. Apollonius wrote in a difficult style (hence his nickname "Dyscolus" or "the Difficult"), but he attempted to expand upon the earlier work of Dionysius Thrax. To the material of the *Tekhne* he added a considerable discussion of sentence analysis or syntax. He and his *Syntax* would become the means of extending the work of the Greek grammarians into the expanding Roman world.[4]

The first one to write a real Latin grammar was Marcus Terentius Varro (116-27 BC), a contemporary of such luminaries as Julius Caesar, Vergil, and

---

[3] Horace, *Epistles*, 2.1. Latium is the ancient name for central Italy, the region where Rome is located.

[4] The word *syntax* comes from a Greek verb meaning "to arrange" or "to put in order." It is used to describe the normal arrangement of a sentence or analysis of that arrangement.

Cicero. Thoroughly educated in the literature of Greece and Rome, he wrote on such divergent topics as mathematics, agriculture, philosophy, law, literature, and language. He wrote a massive work *De Lingua Latina* about 45 BC. This extensive work (twenty-five books long, of which only six survive) presents four groups of words: words with case (nouns, pronouns, and adjectives), words with tense (verbs), words with case and tense (participles), and words with neither (adverbs, prepositions, conjunctions, interjections). Though he is writing about Latin rather than Greek, Varro is clearly using the earlier works of Dionysius Thrax and Apollonius Dyscolus.

However, it was Aelius Donatus, a Roman scholar of the fourth century AD, who took the next step in the transmission of the Greek grammatical tradition. A teacher in Rome (a teacher, by the way, of Jerome, the translator of the Vulgate, the famous Latin version of the Bible), Donatus wrote a two-part Latin grammar, the second part of which came to be known as the *Donati de Partibus Orationis Ars Minor* (*Donatus's Lesser Study of the Parts of Speech*) or simply the *Ars Minor*. In the form of a catechism (i.e., with questions and answers), the little book dealt with the eight parts of speech. Donatus lists them as the noun, pronoun, verb, adverb, participle, conjunction, preposition, and interjection. (Notice that he has left out articles entirely—since there are none in Latin—putting interjections in their place. Note also that he is still listing participles as a part of speech and still discussing adjectives as forms of nouns.) Each time the student confronts a word during sentence analysis, Donatus has him ask, "Quae pars orationis est?" ("What part of speech is it?")[5] This is the origin of the method of sentence analysis called "parsing," which would be used in traditional grammar from then on. Another work by him, his *Ars Grammatica*, was a more thorough-going work on the literary art, but it was his *Ars Minor* that served as the next link in the chain of Western grammar.

Just as Greek had been a necessary foreign language to the Romans, so Latin became a necessity for anyone in the Roman Empire who wished to succeed. Eventually there were Latin grammars written for these non-native speakers, especially in places like Palestine, North Africa, and Constantinople. One of these was the work of Priscianus Caesariensis (called Priscian in English), a Christian Roman who lived in the fifth century. Though a native of North Africa, Priscian became famous as a teacher of grammar in Constantinople. He wrote three works on grammar which had a tremendous influence. The first is the *Institutio de Nomine et Pronomine et Verbo* (*A Study of the Noun, Pronoun, and Verb*), a very brief grammatical handbook dealing with those Latin forms which take different inflections to indicate their different usages. Another work of his was the *Partitiones Duodecim Versuum Aeneido Principalium* (*The Parsing of the First Twelve Lines in the "Aeneid"*), which, as its title reveals, is a thorough

[5] Cf. Wayland Chase, *The "Ars Minor" of Donatus* (Madison: University of Wisconsin, 1926).

analysis of the syntax of the opening twelve lines of Vergil's famous epic poem the *Aeneid*. His *Institutio Grammaticae* (*Study of Grammar*) is a lengthy work of eighteen books (about a thousand pages long). It draws largely from Donatus and gives a thorough explanation of everything pertaining to Latin grammar. It might be noted that his many examples are drawn from Latin literature; clearly he—like the earlier Greek and Latin grammarians—understood grammar as intricately connected with literature. The last two books of this work (based on the earlier work of Apollonius Dyscolus) deal with syntax.

The Middle Ages

By the time of Priscian in the fifth century, the Roman Empire was increasingly divided into East and West, and the Western Empire was especially threatened by the invasion of the Germanic barbarians. By the death of the last Roman emperor in 476, the Roman Empire in the West was gradually sinking into what some would later call the "Dark Ages." The barbarian invasions especially led to an incredible decline in education throughout the Roman world. Unlike the attitude evinced by the Romans to the conquered Greeks, these invaders were not interested in acquiring Latin civilization. Over time, there were fewer schools, fewer teachers, fewer scholars, fewer writers, fewer books, and fewer artists. True, some ancient learning was preserved, especially by the monks in the monasteries that sprang up throughout the old empire. But who knows how much was lost? Surely, many works were lost never to be retrieved: an irreparable loss to mankind.

It was not until the ninth century that the West began to emerge from the chaos. Charlemagne ("Charles the Great"), who had united many of the old Roman provinces in Europe under his control, was crowned "Emperor of the Romans" on Christmas Day, 800. But his title was a hollow one. He did not control all of the former Roman Empire, and many of his subjects were barely Roman in culture and education. Nevertheless, Charlemagne did surround himself with educated statesmen, scholars, and churchmen. The blossoming civilization that issued from his capital and school at Aachen (in modern Germany) came to be referred to as the Carolingian Renaissance (from *Carolus*, the Latin form of the name *Charles*). One of the subjects that received a new life under Charlemagne was grammar.

In the early Middle Ages (ca. 500-800) many Latin grammars were written. As the general Latin culture declined, those who wished to hold on to it increasingly needed grammatical instruction. Most grammars written at the time were for non-native speakers (with the changes in the regional varieties of vulgar or common Latin—changes which would eventually result in French, Rumanian, Italian, Portuguese, Spanish, etc.—there were fewer and fewer native Latin speakers), and most of these grammars relied heavily on Donatus.

(Indeed, throughout the Middle Ages any small handbook, grammatical or otherwise, was called a "donat," and any beginner in grammar—or, later, in anything else—was called a "donatist." During the height of the Middle Ages (ca. 800-1100) initiated by the reign of Charlemagne, the works of Priscian were rediscovered. There was a rebirth of interest in sentence analysis and parsing, leading to a cultivation of excellent Latin. Scholars tried to write correctly, powerfully, and elegantly.

In England, the situation was much as in the rest of Europe. Some very small Latin influence remained from the time when the island was the Roman province of Britannia, but the invasion of the Angles, Saxons, Jutes, and Frisians (beginning in 449) produced a decidedly Germanic, pagan culture. The Celts and their Celtic Christianity were forced to the margins of the island and its culture. The arrival of Augustine in 597 as a Roman Catholic missionary led to renewed interest in Latin and its grammar. The great scholar Alcuin (ca. 735-804), who was summoned by Charlemagne to his school at Aachen, wrote a rather popular version of Priscian's grammar, entitled *Dialogus Franconis et Saxonis de Octo Partibus Orationis* (*A Dialogue between a Frank and a Saxon on the Eight Parts of Speech*). From 449 until after the Norman invasion in 1066, English was the language of the land that came to be called England ("Angle-land"). Aelfric (ca. 955-ca. 1050), about a hundred years before the Norman Conquest even wrote a Latin grammar in Old English. *Excerptiones de Arte Grammatica Anglice* (*Excerpts from the Grammatic Art Englished*) is based on an earlier abbreviation of Priscian's *Institutiones Grammaticae* entitled *Excerptiones de Prisciano*. Aelfric translated this work into the English vernacular of his native Wessex, also the home of the famous King Alfred. Though of course this was a book on Latin grammar not English grammar, the use of English in grammatical instruction surely gave impetus to knowledge of English grammar. Technically, Latin was being taught in the medieval English grammar schools; nevertheless, instruction in English grammar occurred informally (much as it still does in Latin classes today): students learned English grammar as a by-product of their study of Latin grammar. Indeed, in his preface, Aelfric says that his work could be used as an introduction to the study of either Latin or English.

This flowering of revitalized medieval Christian culture was marked by the rise of universities throughout Europe. These became centers of a renewed interest in the liberal arts. The ancient Greeks had said that students could not undertake the study of philosophy until they had completed the *enkuklios paideia* or "the rounded education" (the origin of the Latin term *encyclopaedia*).[6] This "rounded education" included grammar, rhetoric, logic, arithmetic, geometry, music, and astronomy. Later, the Romans called these subjects the seven *artes liberales* ("the liberal arts"). (In this context *liberal* probably means "pertaining to a freeman" as opposed to a slave or perhaps even "freeing" or "liberating." A slave might be taught a trade or a particular valuable craft or skill, but a *liber*, a freeman—in order to take his place in the political and cultural life of the Republic—needed not merely a vocational education but an education in the humanities.) The seven liberal arts were divided into the trivium (consisting of grammar, rhetoric, and logic) and the quadrivium (consisting of arithmetic, music, geometry, and astronomy). Grammar thus was seen as one of the three main subjects which were preparatory for all further education. The new European universities hearkened back to the old *enkuklios paideia* of the Greeks and the *artes liberales* of the Romans. They declared as their goal the cultivation of the *universitas* or the whole of Christian learning.

It is interesting to notice the recurring connection between grammar and literature. Cultures that are interested in books and writing (literature) are also interested in grammar. These are intricately intertwined. Without grammar readers can not interpret or understand literature, and it is through grammar that the author expresses his own thoughts in *litterae* (in "letters," in writing) so that they can be understood. In ancient Greece it was the *Iliad* and the *Odyssey* that prompted a study of grammar and literary criticism; in ancient Rome, the Greek and Latin classics; in the Middle Ages, the Bible and the works of the Church fathers (as well as such Greek and Latin classics as they possessed); in the Muslim world, the Qur'an. In the post-Reformation world of

---

[6] The fifth-century AD Greek anthologist Stobaeus cites Crantor, an early follower of Plato. According to Stobaeus, Crantor referred to the studies that must precede the study of philosophy as the "enkuklios paideia." Cf. Stobaeus, *Anthologium*, 2.31.27. There is some debate as to what this expression actually means. Literally, it means the "rounded education." Does that mean simply the "course" or "round" of primary education including grammar, rhetoric, and logic? Does it imply that such *paideia* ("instruction" or "education") made a person—as we might say today—"well-rounded"? Like the term *liberal arts*, it is somewhat unclear. The Roman writer Seneca later commented on primary education: "Pueriles sunt et aliquid habentes liberalibus simile hae artes, quas 'enkuklios paideia' Graeci, nostri autem 'liberales' vocant." ("These arts pertain to youths and possess some similarity to the liberal arts, which the Greeks call the 'enkuklios paideia,' which we however call the 'liberal arts.'") Cf. Seneca, *Epistles*, 88.23. Isocrates, the fourth-century BC Greek orator (not to be confused with the ancient Greek philosopher Socrates), said of such primary education: "When children have worked hard at grammar, music, and the rest of education, they have not yet made progress in speaking better or in deliberating on public affairs, although they have become better prepared to learn the greater and more serious subjects." Literally, he said that the study of grammar (and the rest of the "enkuklios paideia") prepares students to be *eumathesteroi* or "better learners." Cf. Isocrates, *Antidosis*, 267. *Isocrates I*, David Mirhady and Yun Lee Too, trans. (Austin: University of Texas Press, 2000), 253; David Mulroy, *The War against Grammar* (Portsmouth, NH: Boynton/Cook, 2003), 35.

Germany, the Netherlands, England, Scotland, and America, it would be the vernacular Bible. Wherever men are interested in literature, they have to be interested in grammar. If learning from literature is their goal, then learning by means of grammar must be their method.

Note also that knowledge was not confined merely to that which could be discovered through scientific experimentation; it was also learned by contemplation and introspection. Man, they believed, came into the world with *a priori* knowledge, innate ideas and concepts. Socrates, as presented in the dialogues of Plato (Socrates himself wrote nothing), believed that such ideas indicated a pre-birth existence of some kind. Christians believed that these innate ideas were the result rather of divine creation. Man, because of his creation by the hand of God, bore the *imago Dei* ("the image of God"). One manifestation of the divine image was language and thought, expressed through grammar. Since man as man was marked by the capacity for language and thought, it was through grammar that man could come to understand his own thoughts and the thoughts of others. Grammar was the *alma mater* (the "nourishing mother") of any educated person, the first of the liberal arts. Personified Grammar is frequently depicted in allegorical medieval art. Sometimes she is a lady, like Lady Wisdom in the book of Proverbs. Above the West Portal of Chartres Cathedral, a personified Grammatica is located with the other liberal arts.

As the Carolingian Renaissance waned and the Middle Ages dragged out to an ignominious conclusion (ca. 1100-1500), Latin classroom instruction ceased to emphasize sentence analysis and parsing. Syntax—and its connections with the great works of classical and medieval literature—was replaced with a smattering of poorly understood phrases and mottoes. Latin ceased to be a tool for serious education and became a decorative technique for would-be scholastics. Late medieval Latin is infamous for its inaccuracies and errors. The unfortunate development of scholasticism took over much or most of European education and learning, even overwhelming the universities. Logic was raised above grammar. Instead of mastering Latin grammar and composition, instead of reading the classical works of literature carefully and thoughtfully, analyzing their meaning and import, scholastics focused on precise, even narrow questions of logic. Logic came to surpass grammar, philosophy, and even theology in importance. While the Greek "rounded education" and the Roman liberal arts and the medieval Christian education emphasized the true, the good, and the beautiful, scholasticism forsook that emphasis. Soon the great classical authors, the Church fathers, even the Bible itself were being generally neglected; with the neglect of literature there was the concomitant neglect of grammar. There were a few places that held on to traditional grammar (like the universities at Orleans and Chartres in France), but they were few. The

English scholar John of Salisbury (d. 1180) described the sad state of affairs under scholasticism like this: "Later, ... popular opinion veered away from the truth, when men preferred to seem, rather than to be, philosophers. ... Since then, less time and attention have been given to the study of grammar. As a result, we find men who profess all the arts, liberal and mechanical, but who are ignorant of this very first one, without which it is futile to go on to attempt the others. ... Grammar alone has the unique privilege of making one 'lettered.' ... Anyone who spurns grammar, is not only not a 'teacher of letters,' but does not even deserve to be called 'lettered.'"[7] The study of grammar was at a low ebb.

The Renaissance

Eventually, the advocates of the old humanities, the humanists as they came to be called, rebelled against scholasticism. Francesco Petrarch, in Italy, and his fellow humanists took their name from a passage in Cicero's *Pro Archia*: "studiis humanitatis ac litterarum" ("the studies of humanity and letters").[8] From its beginning the Renaissance produced changes in all the humanities, including the area of "letters" or grammar. If they were going to replace scholasticism with humanism, if they were going to recapture the ancient civilization of Greece and Rome, and the Christian culture of the past, they had to rediscover literature and grammar. This rediscovery of Latin—and, later, Greek—literature necessarily gave a renewed impetus to traditional grammar. The practice of sentence analysis revived, and emphasis was put on writing correctly, thoughtfully, and elegantly like the ancients. Thus, the Renaissance produced massive changes not only in the visual arts but also in the study of language and literature.

With its renewed interest in the classical world and its culture, the Renaissance necessarily produced a renewal of interest in the grammars of ancient Greek and Latin. When Constantinople fell to the Muslim Turks in 1453, many scholars in the Eastern Empire fled west, particularly to Italy. By 1476 a grammar of ancient Greek had been produced in Milan by Manuel Chrysolaras, the first Byzantine scholar to come to Italy. Not surprisingly, this renewed interest in Greek led to a renewed interest in the Greek New Testament. Desiderius Erasmus traveled around Europe searching for old Biblical manuscripts in Greek. He compiled about a dozen such manuscripts into a Greek New Testament, which he published in 1516. The importance of this work cannot be overstated. It led immediately to calls for new translations

[7] John of Salisbury, *The Metalogicon of John of Salisbury, A Twelfth-Century Defense of the Verbal and Logical Arts of the Trivium*, trans. Daniel D. McGarry (Berkeley: University of California, 1955), 71 (I.24); Mulroy, 48-49. This is an important work for anyone interested in the value of traditional grammar and its connections with liberal education.

[8] Cicero, *Pro Archia*, 3.

of the Bible into the languages of Europe. This interest in the vernacular Bible intersected nicely with the growth of Protestantism. In England, a vernacular New Testament, newly translated by William Tyndale, appeared in 1526. After Tyndale's arrest (and subsequent death at the stake), Miles Coverdale compiled an entire English Bible in 1535. These were followed by a succession of English Bibles: the Matthew's Bible, the Great Bible, the Geneva Bible, the Bishops' Bible, and the King James Bible.

Interestingly, this renewal of interest in the languages of Greek and Latin had a profound effect on the vernacular languages of Europe. As they learned to appreciate the beauty and excellence of those ancient languages, they were struck by the need to encourage beauty and excellence in their own vernacular tongues. Eloquence, surely, was not to be limited to the past. The cry throughout Europe was "ad fontes!" ("to the fountains" or "to the springs"). The humanists wanted to look again at the literature and arts of the ancient world, the original springs from which Western culture had flowed. But they did not want to remain there. They wanted to take that knowledge and apply it to every facet of life. They saw their entire culture as having a *renaissance* (French for "new birth"), and they wanted it to grow into a beautiful, glorious culture. One aspect of this was language and grammar.

Grammar, the key for acquiring the knowledge of the ancient Greeks and Romans, became important again. In the preface to his book *The Praise of Folly*, Erasmus condemned the ignorant scholastic schoolmasters: "They cram their pupils with utter nonsense ... but ... Donatus, do they not scorn in comparison with themselves!"[9] Erasmus saw that a return to sources meant a return to the study of grammar. When Johannes Gutenberg set up his new printing press with movable type, the first book off the press was the Bible, but the second was Donatus's *Ars Minor*. Latin grammars written in vernacular European languages soon followed. Already in the fifteenth century John Leyland had written a three-part work on Latin grammar in English. Though, like Aelfric's earlier work, it was intended to teach Latin, clearly there was a great deal of English being taught as well. When William Caxton's printing press was set up in London in 1477, Leyland's work was published and widely used. Soon there were Latin grammars available in Europe in Spanish (1481), French (1514), and German (1525), the last by Martin Luther's protégé Philip Melanchthon.

John Colet, the dean of St. Paul's Cathedral in London and the son of the wealthy lord mayor of London, determined to start a new school for the advancement of humane learning in England. In 1509 he established St. Paul's

[9] Desiderius Erasmus, *The Praise of Folly*, Hoyt Hopewell Hudson, trans. (NY: The Modern Library, 1941), 71.

School, in London, and chose William Lily as its first headmaster. The school, which emphasized grammar and classical literature, needed a proper grammar book. Using an earlier work by Colet, Lily composed such a grammar book, which was then amended by Erasmus and added to by Colet. It was truly a cooperative work; all three must be considered its authors. *A Short Introduction of Grammar* was published by 1542 under decree by Henry VIII as the official, royal Latin grammar book. "Lily's Grammar" (as it came to be called) reformed the teaching of Latin in England. However, though its primary goal was improved instruction in Latin, one of its beneficial effects was increased understanding of English. Indeed, this seems to have been a secondary goal of the work. Latin examples are followed by English translations, and sometimes advice is given that will be applicable to English grammar as well as Latin. For example, in the explanation of translating an English sentence into Latin, it says: "When an English [sentence] is given to be made in Latin, look out the principal verb." In another instance, it says, "Whan ye have found the verb, aske this question, *who*, or *what*, and that woorde that aunswereth to the question, shall bee the nominative case to the verbe." [sic][10] This grammar book had the result of educating an entire new generation of English schoolboys in the grammar of, first, Latin, and then English. Some of the young scholars who learned grammar from Lily, Colet, and Erasmus were Edmund Spenser, Christopher Marlowe, William Shakespeare, Ben Jonson, and Francis Bacon, some of the preeminent writers of the language.

The new interest in the vernacular affected every European language. A grammar of Italian was produced in 1441; of Spanish, in 1492; of French, in 1530; of Bohemian (Czech), in 1533; of Portuguese, in 1536; of Welsh, in 1567; of Polish, in 1568; of German, in 1573; and of Dutch, in 1584. However, it was not until 1586 that an English grammar was written.

The first grammar of the English language *in* the English language was written by William Bullokar, a retired soldier and amateur scholar. He evidently published his *Brief Grammar for English* in 1586. Only two copies survive. On the copy in the Bodleian Library at Oxford University, the author has evidently written, "This is the first grammar for English that ever was printed, except my Grammar at large."[11] That "Grammar at large" was perhaps an earlier grammar that was not printed, or else it has now been totally lost. Unfortunately, Bullokar was keenly interested in spelling reform, and his book was printed using his revised, newfangled spelling. This unfortunately doomed it to obscurity.

---

[10] William Lily and John Colet, *A Short Introduction of Grammar, 1549* (Menston, UK: The Scolar Press Ltd., 1970), r. 24.

[11] Diane Bornstein, intro., *William Bullokar, Booke at Large (1580) and Bref Grammar for English (1586)* (Delmar, NY: Scholars' Facsimiles & Reprints, 1977), x.

Soon, many other English grammars followed. Even such writers as Ben Jonson and John Milton produced English grammars. From 1700 to 1750, fifty were published; between 1750 and 1800, two hundred.

It was not merely the countries of Western Europe that benefited from the burgeoning Renaissance interest in grammar. The exploration of vernacular grammars intersected wonderfully the advancing exploration of parts of the world that had previously been little known or entirely unknown to Europeans. A grammar of the Ethiopian language was produced by a European in 1552, Quechuan (Peruvian Indian) in 1560, Japanese in 1604, Malay in 1612, Turkish in 1612, Persian in 1639, Vietnamese in 1651, Massachusett Indian in 1666 (by the Puritans), Chinese in 1703, Urdu in 1741, Innuit (Eskimo) in 1760, Bengali in 1778, and Kurdish in 1787. To some degree, interest in vernacular grammar early on became connected with the Christian missionary enterprise as well.

The Rise of Standard English

Language studies in the eighteenth century were marked by a desire for standardization. This desire for an ordered and stable language had been rising for some time. The invention of the printing press with movable type had affected all of Europe, and England was no exception. After William Caxton set up his printing press in 1477, the number of books in circulation obviously increased tremendously. Different printers using different spellings, different punctuations, and different grammatical constructions led to a certain amount of chaos. Though one can admire the amazing fluidity of the language during the Renaissance, a time when many new words were being coined and writers felt free to use language in new and unusual ways, nevertheless such freedom and variety could be hindrances to communication.

Also, the very ethos of the time moved grammarians in the direction of a more standardized language. During the sixteenth and seventeenth centuries English life had been decidedly tumultuous. Religiously, England had experienced the break with the Roman Catholic Church under Henry VIII, had established a very Protestant Church of England under his son Edward VI, had returned to Catholicism under Queen Mary, and had attempted a *via media* under Elizabeth I. The rise of Puritanism in the seventeenth century and the conflicts between the Stuart monarchs and Parliament led ultimately to the English Civil War (1642-49) and the execution of Charles I in 1649, then the restoration of the monarchy in 1660, then the ouster of James II in the "Glorious Revolution" of 1688. For about two hundred years, English life had been characterized by change, conflict, and tumult. By the eighteenth century, the British wanted stability, peace, and calm. The increased interest in classical culture which had begun in the Renaissance was also strong in the eighteenth century. When scholars looked at Greek and Latin they found languages which seemed to them logical and orderly and stable—just the things which they felt were missing from their own language. (Of course, had they seen Greek and Latin when they were still living languages, which were necessarily changing, they might have thought about these matters differently, but by this time classical Greek and Latin were no longer living languages.) In various ways, politically, philosophically, religiously, even aesthetically, the eighteenth century was a conservative period in English life, looking back to the grace and elegance of ancient Greek and Roman culture.

Nor was this ethos limited to England. Italy and France had already established academies of scholars to govern and standardize their languages. Their academies limited the invention of new words and attempted to regularize spelling and grammar. There were those in England, like the writers Daniel Defoe, Jonathan Swift, and Joseph Addison, who wished for an English academy to standardize the English language as well. Swift, in fact, wrote a famous pamphlet entitled *A Proposal for Correcting, Improving, and Ascertaining the English Tongue*. However, other views prevailed. Standardization was left to Samuel Johnson and his *Dictionary of the English Language* (1755) and to the grammarians of the period.

Beginning about the middle of the eighteenth century there was a sudden new interest in English grammar. Joseph Priestley, the noted scientist, published *The Rudiments of English Grammar* in 1761. [By the way, it was Priestley's grammar that finally separated adjectives from nouns and dropped participles as a part of speech. Priestley's eight categories have been used ever since.] Robert Lowth, the bishop of London, wrote his *Short Introduction to English Grammar*, published in 1762. One of the most widely-used grammars in England was *English Grammar Adapted to Different Classes of Learners*, written in 1795 by Lindley Murray. Murray, from an American Quaker family in Philadelphia, had retired to rural England as a semi-invalid. It was there that he wrote his grammar book for a nearby Quaker school for girls. It became extremely popular, selling over a million copies by 1850. In America, Noah Webster in 1784 published *A Grammatical Institute of the English Language*, which eventually became his *American Spelling Book*, the famous "blue-backed speller" used by thousands of American children in the nineteenth century. Webster followed this in 1828 with *An American Dictionary of the English Language*, the first American dictionary.

For the first time in the history of the English language, the study of English grammar became a regular part of grammar school education. Joseph

Priestley, in his grammar book, urged teachers to set aside time in their school classes for instruction in English grammar, usage, and composition.[12]

The rise of philosophical interest in grammar and language went hand-in-hand with the new interest in grammatical correctness. There was a growing interest in "natural grammar" and comparative philology. This is, for example, the period that produced Sir William Jones and his famous paper recognizing the similarities between Latin and Sanskrit and suggesting the existence of an early ancestral Indo-European language. The desire for grammatical knowledge manifested itself in two ways. Classroom teachers wanted to teach their students "proper" or correct English grammar; hence, they compiled various grammars that attempted to define such correctness (usually based on the writings of the famous English authors of the period). Others explored the connections between all languages.

Some have criticized the period of the eighteenth and early nineteenth centuries as a period of "prescriptivist" grammar, with self-appointed authorities proscribing certain spelling or grammatical constructions and prescribing others.[13] Certainly, there is some basis for this criticism. Few in this period had much knowledge of or appreciation for the history of the English language. Old English and Middle English, with all their many changes in inflection and usage, were just beginning to be studied in a scholarly way. The eighteenth century did suffer from a certain amount of stuffy self-righteousness in the area of language and literature. As a result, some things came to be considered incorrect which had been considered correct for centuries (for example, the wonderful old double negative). The period, to some extent, did create a rather artificial standardized language to fit the increasingly standardized world of the Industrial Revolution. Surely errors were made by overzealous schoolmasters who had little understanding of how the English language had developed.

On the other hand, was this increased interest in grammar and usage merely window dressing, merely preparing students so that they could move up the social ladder to capitalist success? Some would say so. Some would condemn the entire movement as "prescriptivist" and overly rule-bound. But is it not possible that it was a manifestation of something more substantial, a recognition of the value of excellence? Does prescriptive grammar not have some moral or even theological component? It clearly does. It values tradition; it values logic; it recognizes the innate language capabilities of man as a manifestation of the *imago Dei*; it recognizes the importance of beauty, order,

---

[12] Joseph Priestley, *The Rudiments of English Grammar 1761* (Menston, UK: The Scolar Press Ltd., 1969), ix.

[13] To proscribe is to forbid or condemn; to prescribe is to require or direct.

and excellence; it values charity for one's neighbor which will manifest itself in a concern for communication; and it certainly is connected with an appreciation of the *logos*—whether that is the logos of Holy Scripture or even the logos of Shakespeare or the U.S. Constitution. Because cultural traditionalists value precise communication, they value grammar. This is, of course, necessarily connected with their interest in the correct understanding of the Bible and of all other important works (from the ancient Greek and Roman classics to the Church fathers to Aquinas to Shakespeare to the Founding Fathers and the Constitution).

Of course, these matters *are* social conventions in some sense. Maintaining traditional grammar is not the exact equivalent of preserving the Decalogue. Surely, however, there is a place for thoughtful attention to one's language. Since English does not have an academy, its governor must be the consensus of educated opinion, the usage of the greatest and most thoughtful writers and scholars. In some ways this reflects the growing influence of the common man. The standard of English speech (both in Great Britain and America) is not the aristocracy or the royal court or even rich people or celebrities; the aristocracy has been replaced by a "meritocracy" of those who truly care about the language.

Admittedly, some of the prescriptivists (at least a few) were trying to "freeze" the language to keep it from continuing to change. That is, of course, a useless task, like King Canute's commanding the tide to stand still. Others, however, were trying to explore whether there were not some form of English which is more traditional or more logical or more "correct" than others. What they were grappling with was the tension between correctness and inevitable language change. Surely it is a good thing to reflect on how one should speak and write, just as it is good to reflect on how one should behave in other ways (in eating or in dressing or in all sorts of ways). Surely there is a place for etiquette. If so, then there is a place for "prescriptive grammar" which some have pejoratively labeled as "language etiquette."

One fair criticism of certain grammarians (especially in the late nineteenth and early twentieth centuries) was the emphasis on rules and the abandonment of sentence analysis. Grammar is more than the study of rules; it is, as Robert Einarsson says, the search for "the underlying principles and patterns that make language work."[14] It is more than mere rules. In 1907 Edwin Woolley published his *Handbook of Composition: A Compendium of Rules Regarding Good English, Grammar, Sentence Structure, Paragraphing, Manuscript*

[14] Robert Einarsson, "The Place of Grammar in the Language Arts Curriculum"; http:/www.classiclanguagearts.net/resources/re-paper-elac.html; October 6, 2005; accessed May, 2007.

Arrangement, Punctuation, Spelling, Essay Writing, and Letter Writing, which contains 350 numbered rules! Surely that is not the best way of approaching grammar.

On the other hand, even late in the nineteenth century there were still important developments in the teaching of traditional grammar. In the 1870s, Alonzo Reed and Brainerd Kellogg, teachers at Brooklyn Collegiate and Polytechnic Institute in New York, developed an excellent system of sentence diagraming that is still widely used by traditional grammarians today. Their diagrams help to facilitate sentence analysis (syntax), making it clear, accurate, and understandable. (The diagrams in this book are based on those of Reed and Kellogg.)

The Rise of Linguistics

Admittedly, as early as the seventeenth century the unified worldview of the West, especially as manifested in the Renaissance-Reformation consensus in Northern Europe, had begun to manifest certain cracks. "'Tis all in pieces, all coherence gone," wrote John Donne.[15] In the eighteenth and nineteenth centuries, these cracks began to turn into fissures. The so-called Enlightenment emphasized rationality, logic, order, almost to the exclusion of emotion. It came to give primacy to empirical evidence. The Romantic Movement emphasized freedom, spontaneity, and emotion; it rejected empiricism, but also reason. The worldview of the West had certainly undergone change in its development since the classical period. It had been affected by Christianity, by the fall of the Roman Empire, by medieval theology, by the Renaissance and the Reformation. Nevertheless, prior to the Enlightenment, Western thought—despite certain competing religious and political views—presented an amazingly united front. However, as the pendulum swung first to the Enlightenment and then to Romanticism, the coherence of Western thought began to fail. Western culture began to develop in ways far removed from the philosophical and theological origins of its tradition.

This abandonment of tradition was accelerated by various manifestations of modernism beginning in the mid-nineteenth century. Building on the foundation of the empiricism of the Enlightenment, modernism emphasized scientific thought to the absolute exclusion of all other methods of knowledge. One of the most influential changes involved the origin of man himself. In 1859 Charles Darwin published his study entitled *The Origin of Species*. The implications of Darwinism were felt not merely in biology and the sciences but in every area of thought. It may be surprising to some to consider that

[15] John Donne, "The First Anniversary: An Anatomy of the World," *The New Oxford Book of Seventeenth-Century Verse*, ed. Alastair Fowler (Oxford: Oxford University, 1992), 113.

Darwinian evolutionary ideas would have any effect on the study of grammar. From its very origins, Western thought had believed in innate ideas. Whether they believed in some pre-existent state (like Socrates) or in divine creation by God, Western thinkers believed that human beings were born with certain "gifts." One of these gifts was language and thought. The entire history of traditional grammar–from the Greeks to the Romans to the early Christians to the medievals to the humanists of the Renaissance and Reformation to the eighteenth-century grammarians–had involved a consideration of the innate concepts of language embedded in the human mind. Grammar was simply a manifestation of the Hellenic-Hebraic-Christian philosophy of language. After Darwin, however, all was different. Man was not a creation of a Divine Creator; man was merely the result of a concatenation of chance developments. Noah Webster, in the preface to his *American Dictionary*, had summed up the earlier view of language: "We may infer that language was bestowed on Adam, in the same manner as all his other faculties and knowledge, by supernatural power; or, in other words, was of divine origin. ... Language, as well as the faculty of speech, was the immediate gift of God."[16] Darwinism undermined this view of language.

Darwinism did not allow for a world of Divine Creation. A virulent scientism replaced reason. Darwinism produced an intellectual culture which was naturalistic (non-supernatural), materialistic (non-spiritual), and scientistic (non-rational). Philology (the love of the logos) and traditional grammar came to be replaced with linguistics. The study of language, like virtually every subject, was greatly influenced by the new scientism, the approach which stressed the empirical nature of learning. Reason (based on the acceptance of *a priori* assumptions) was rejected in favor of experimentation, even in the areas of life which heretofore had been untouched by experimental science, areas such as theology, education, and language. These new approaches rejected all non-empirical (non-experimental) knowledge no matter how ancient nor how reasonable or wise and raised the scientific method to a place of total primacy. Hence, it is appropriate to call these efforts not merely science but scientism; it is the belief in the absolute superiority of science over all other methods of knowledge.

These new views affected the teaching of grammar in two ways. First, they changed the way that teachers approached the idea of instruction. Many who accepted modernist views referred to themselves as progressives. Many progressives advocated drastic changes in government, education, and culture generally. They called, for example, for abandonment of traditional methods in

[16] Noah Webster, "Introduction" to *An American Dictionary of the English Language* (Springfield, MA: George and Charles Merriam, 1855), xxiii.

the school classroom. Grammar, history, and geography were merely abstractions which should be jettisoned by the new progressive teacher. The child (who was the new focus in the new progressive classroom) was not interested in those boring subjects but in "the real world." Among the progressives, the works of John Dewey, William James, and Herbert Spencer were particularly influential. Edward Thorndike in his influential textbook *Educational Psychology* swept away all earlier views of the nature of man. The Biblical view was that man was created in the image of God (the *imago Dei*) and hence had such qualities as a spiritual nature, a free will, and language and thought. This high view of man's place as the supreme creation of God was accompanied by the belief in the Fall. Man has sinned; he has disobeyed a holy God, and the resultant Fall has affected him and all creation. According to the Christian view, all mankind are born spiritually deformed and sinful (Original Sin) and proceed to sin actually in thought, word, and deed. But Thorndike, like the other Social Darwinists, discarded these ancient understandings.

Next, the implications of Darwinism affected the study of language. Beginning in the 1870s, the "neogrammarians" at the University of Leipzig in Germany began to explore how language was produced in the mind and in speech. This was a decided departure from traditional grammar and philology. In effect, linguistics was a branch of the new science of anthropology.

In the new field of linguistics, the first theory came to be called structural grammar (or immediate constituent grammar). Ferdinand de Saussure (1857-1913), the Swiss linguist, introduced the idea. Later it was refined by such figures as Leonard Bloomfield (*Language*, 1933) and Zellig Harris (*Methods in Structural Linguistics*, 1951). Saussure tried to explain the difference between what he called *parole* ("speech"), the actual words that people speak, and *langue* ("language"), the knowledge of language that speakers learn from their language communities. This separation of grammar from the actual speech of people (much less from the writings of people, and even less from the writings of the great canonical authors) led to a complete break between the world of the classroom and the world of linguistics. Linguistics was interested in *langue*, but classroom teachers were interested in *parole*. As linguistics continued to develop as a science based on empirical evidence, it spun further and further away from traditional classroom grammar. Linguistics became more and more incomprehensible for the layman (even the educated layman), and classroom grammar eventually became the preserve merely of stubborn traditionalists or else began to disappear completely.

One of the important structuralists was Charles Fries (1887-1967). In his influential book *The Structure of English* Fries criticized traditional grammar for assuming that certain things were "intuitive." He sought, he said, to make grammar more "explicit" and more "empirical." He made his view immediately clear on the first page of his book: "The reader should know, first of all, that he will *not* find in this book the usual analysis of sentences that pupils have struggled with and the schools have taught for more than a hundred and fifty years. Modern scientific study has freed us to abandon many of the older commonly held views of language and has provided us with new principles and new assumptions which underlie new methods of analysis and verification." He lamented that "the views and practices of a prescientific era still dominate[d] the schools." "The conventional 'formal grammar,'" he said, "is like the Ptolemaic astronomy, falsely oriented. The study of the usual 'formal grammar,' then, has much the same sort of value and usefulness as the study of the astronomy of Ptolemy, or of the medical beliefs and practices of Galen, the great Greek physician. Being falsely oriented, 'formal grammar,' as it is studied in relation to English, cannot be expected to provide any satisfactory insight into the mechanisms of our language or any grasp of the processes by which language functions." According to Fries, traditional grammar has as much modern relevance as the idea of the flat earth or alchemy. He despaired over those "who have not grasped the thoroughly different basic orientation of the modern scientific approach to language" and who "suggest that pupils begin the study of grammar with the materials of the traditional 'formal grammar.'"[17] Fries rejected the eight parts of speech in favor of four "classes" (noun, verb, adjective, and adverb) and nineteen (!) groups of "function words" (including such items as *here* and *there*, *yes* and *no*, *let's*, *please*, forms of *do*, etc.).

In 1957 Noam Chomsky (1928-) issued a work which differed from Fries and his structuralists. Chomsky's *Syntactic Structures* was, in some ways, a step back toward the traditional world. He recognized that there was a "universal grammar" common to all human beings; this sounded much like some in the eighteenth century. But Chomsky, being a thorough-going Darwinian (as well as a Marxist), saw this not as an innate idea planted by a Creator (as the eighteenth-century philosophers did) but merely as a "language acquisition device" connected with certain features of the human brain.

The grammatical theory that Chomsky developed focused not on sentences in literature and not really on everyday speech. Rather, he sought to understand how language was formed in the brain. For instance, he attempted to formulate rules which would explain how a speaker—in his brain—turns a statement into a question. Whereas traditional grammar, focused as it was on the written sentence, gave particular attention to "letters" or literature, Chomsky's grammar was really a scientific exploration of the human brain. He wanted

[17] Charles Carpenter Fries, *The Structure of English* (NY: Harcourt, Brace & World, Inc., 1952), 1, 277.

to describe how what he called the "deep structure" in the brain turned into the actual spoken words, which he called the "surface structure." Because his grammatical method focused on how deep structural forms were transformed into surface structural forms, it was sometimes called transformational grammar. Because it sought to explain how sentences were produced or "generated," it was sometimes called generative grammar. (Sometimes it went by both names; sometimes it has been referred to merely as "T-G.")

Needless to say, Chomsky's linguistic interests are far removed from the tradition that prevailed, more or less successfully, from the ancient world into the nineteenth century. Also, it should be noted that even Chomsky himself recognized the value of students' obtaining a knowledge of traditional grammar, not transformational grammar: "I think that it [traditional grammar] should be taught for its own intrinsic interest and importance. I don't see how any person can truly be called 'educated' who doesn't know the elements of sentence structure, or who doesn't understand the nature of a relative clause, a passive construction, and so on. Furthermore, if one is going to discuss literature, including here what students write themselves, and to come to understand how it is written and why, these conceptual tools are indispensable." He also said, "I think traditional grammar so-called ... remains today a very impressive and useful basis for such teaching. I can't see any reason for teaching structural grammars of English, or for teaching transformational grammar in the manner of some instructional books that I have seen."[18]

Nevertheless, despite Chomsky's own protestations, some educators leapt on Chomsky's linguistic ideas and declared the teaching of traditional grammar a waste of time and perhaps even positively harmful. For people who had long ago jettisoned such non-scientific beliefs as Divine Creation or Original Sin or other old-fashioned ideas which the ancients and medievals might have labeled as "wisdom," these new ideas served a useful function: they were just more evidence that traditional grammar, like all things traditional, was at the best antique and at the worst tyrannical. Traditional grammar came to be viewed with disdain—along with traditional Christian orthodoxy or traditional social mores or conservative political theory. Commenting on the "new grammar," one linguistician noted that "it was no longer felt to be satisfactory to explain [grammar] at a particular time in terms of abstract principles, but rather in terms of their development from some previous state by adaptation to changing external conditions. The 'providential' theory of history of the general Christian tradition had been increasingly challenged, and was replaced by evolutionary

[18] Noam Chomsky, "Noam Chomsky Writes to Mrs. Davis About Grammar and Education," *English Education*, 16 (October, 1984), 165. Cf. Mulroy, 74.

and secular theories of human development."[19] Another pointed out that modern views of grammar "[warn] us to give up, to abandon entirely the old dogmatic, normative, theological approach of traditional grammar and of social snobbery; and to substitute the relativistic, objective approach of scientific study and analysis."[20] What had earlier been viewed as wise and beautiful was now scornfully rejected with all the other outmoded relics of the past.

The result was that English teachers (who like everyone else had been trained to accept the validity of modern science over the gravity of ancient tradition) first jettisoned traditional grammar in favor of linguistics, then, finding that impossible to explain to students (because they themselves did not understand it well and because there was nothing there to understand), abandoned grammar altogether. Of course, the growth of relativism, which rejected all claims of philosophical and moral truth, simply encouraged the abandonment of grammar. If everything else was up for grabs, if they could not speak authoritatively about the nature of man or the roles of man and woman or the origin of life, if it was wrong to say "That is wrong" about matters which had previously been considered wicked or immoral, then how could one dare to criticize comma splices?

By the 1950s, structural linguistics and generative linguistics began to reach the classroom. Traditional grammar was replaced by the "new grammar." One of the most prominent textbook writers was Paul Roberts. He attempted to translate the work of Charles Fries and then of Noam Chomsky into elementary and secondary English textbooks. His *Patterns of English* (1956) was structuralist; his *English Syntax* (1962) was generative. To students (and to many teachers) they were simply incredibly complicated and indecipherable. Like the "new math" introduced at the same time, the "new grammar" affected the schools tremendously. Traditional grammar had, ever since ancient times, focused on explaining the structure of sentences (especially as expressed in literature by those recognized as the best writers); hence it had both a syntactic emphasis and a usage emphasis. The modern linguistic grammar, with its emphasis on understanding language by means of empirical scientific data, attempted to get "behind" or "above" the actual language and explain how it had been produced in the brain.

---

[19] John Lyons, *Introduction to Theoretical Linguistics* (Cambridge: Cambridge University Press, 1968), 23; cf. James A. Chapman, *What about Transformational Grammar?* (Pensacola, FL: A Beka Book Publications, 1985), 4.

[20] Robert A. Hall, Jr., *Linguistics and Your Language*, second rev. ed. (Garden City, NY: Anchor Books, 1960), 259; cf. Chapman, 4. I cannot overestimate the importance of Professor Chapman's views in the shaping of my own. He served as a mentor to me while we were both working for A Beka Book Publications in the 1970s and 1980s; to him I owe the development of my views on traditional English grammar. His delightful little pamphlet on transformational grammar is particularly insightful about the Darwinian underpinnings of transformational grammar.

Researchers in linguistics cited their own data to prove that traditional grammar was "not just useless but pernicious."[21] Richard Braddock, Richard Lloyd-Jones, and Lowell Schoer in their *Research in Written Composition* (1963) asserted: "The conclusion can be stated in strong and unqualified terms: the teaching of formal grammar has a negligible or, because it usually displaces some instruction and practice in actual composition, even a harmful effect on the improvement in writing."[22] By the 1980s the influence of linguistic grammar was so powerful that the many English teachers involved in the National Council of Teachers of English (NCTE) were virtually entirely converted. In 1985 the NCTE officially resolved "that the use of isolated grammar and usage exercises not supported by theory and research is a deterrent to the improvement of students' speaking and writing and that, in order to improve both of these, class time at all levels must be devoted to opportunities for meaningful listening, speaking, reading, and writing; and that the NCTE urge the discontinuance of testing practices that encourage the teaching of grammar rather than English language arts instruction."[23] George Hillocks, a researcher connected with the NCTE, issued this warning: "School boards, administrators, and teachers who impose the systematic study of traditional school grammar on their students over lengthy periods of time in the name of teaching writing do them a gross disservice which should not be tolerated by anyone concerned with the effective teaching of writing."[24] Traditional grammar had reached a new nadir.

There are some signs for hopefulness. Many conservative schools (some Christian schools, some traditional private schools) and some in the "back-to-basics" movement in the public schools have begun to re-emphasize traditional English grammar. Many involved in home-schooling have re-discovered the grammatical art as well. Various publishers have produced textbooks that teach traditional grammar. In 1998, sensing the same problems as those in the United States, even the British Labour government under Tony Blair made grammatical analysis a renewed focus in its National Literacy Strategy.

---

[21] Mulroy, 6.

[22] Richard Braddock, Richard Lloyd-Jones, and Lowell Schoer, *Research in Written Composition* (Champaign, IL: National Council of Teachers of English, 1963), 37-38.

[23] "NCTE Position Statement on Grammar Exercises to Teach Speaking and Writing" (1985); http://www.ncte.org/about/over/positions/category/gram/107492.htm; accessed May, 2007.

[24] George Hillocks, Jr., *Research on Written Composition: New Directions for Teaching* (Urbana, IL: Clearinghouse on Reading and Communication Skills, National Institute for Education, 1986), 248; cf. George Hillocks, Jr. and Michael W. Smith, "Grammars and Literacy Learning," in *Handbook of Research on Teaching the English Language Arts*, second ed., eds. James Flood et al., 729; cf. Mulroy, 6.

So what should traditionalist grammarians do? Robert Burchfield, the chief editor of the *Oxford English Dictionary*, gives this advice:

> The approach to English grammar in the 20th century—the move toward a kind of logical, mathematical description of the language—has been a disaster, leaving children totally at sea. Schoolmasters are also confused and don't know what to teach. The upshot is that, by some estimates, about 15 percent of all Americans are now functionally illiterate. The schools that I know in Britain that continue to teach grammar and spelling in an old-fashioned way are the ones that produce great scholars and that keep the language going in an effective way. ... The teachers have got to go back to their books and learn what the history of constructions is, and not be ultraconservative. At the same time, they've got to have a framework for teaching grammar. They won't find it among the new school of grammarians who give them no guidance whatever and have yet failed to produce a single grammar that makes sense.[25]

[25] Robert Burchfield, "The English Language Is Changing, Not Going Rotten," *U.S. News & World Report*, 15 December 1980, 71-72.

Chapter 2
The Parts of Speech

Words are classed according to their functions in a particular sentence. As discussed in Chapter 1, the parts of speech were of great interest to the early grammarians. In the *Tekhne Grammatike* of Dionysius Thrax, the eight parts of speech were nouns (including adjectives), verbs, participles, articles, pronouns, prepositions, adverbs (including interjections), and conjunctions. Donatus, in his Latin grammar, used basically the same ones. However, since there are no articles in Latin, that part is missing; also, he separated interjections from adverbs. It was Joseph Priestley, in his *Rudiments of English Grammar* in 1761, who regularized the eight parts of speech into their current form. He included participles with verbs, and included articles with adjectives. Since the seventeenth century, English grammars have recognized eight parts of speech: the verb, the noun, the pronoun, the adjective, the adverb, the preposition, the conjunction, and the interjection.

Verb

A verb frequently indicates an action or helps to make a statement.

> In thy face I *see* the map of honour, truth, and loyalty. –William Shakespeare, *2 Henry VI*
> Now *abideth* faith, hope, charity, these three. –1 Corinthians 13:13

A verb may be used to join the subject and a complement renaming or describing it (a linking verb).

> The earth *is* the Lord's, and the fulness thereof. –Psalm 24:1
> Beauty soon *grows* familiar to the lover. –Joseph Addison

A verb may be used as part of a larger verb form or verb phrase (a helping verb or an auxiliary verb).

> All, all *are sleeping* on the hill. –Edgar Lee Masters
> The inscription *had been carved* on the chimneybreast.

Noun

A noun names a person, place, thing, or idea.

woman (person)
Athens (place)
wheat (thing)
liberty (idea)

A common noun is often preceded by an article (*a, an, the*) or an adjective. A proper noun is a particular person, place, thing, or idea and begins with a capital letter.

a murderer (person)	Macbeth (person)
the country (place)	Mesopotamia (place)
the poem (thing)	"Elegy Written in a Country Churchyard" (thing)
a heresy (idea)	Gnosticism (idea)

A collective noun gives the name of a group (and may be used singularly to refer to the group as a whole or plurally to refer to all the individuals in the group).

faculty	flock
army	herd
committee	jury

The flock was feeding on the hillside. (singular)
The flock were all running in different directions. (plural)

A compound noun is composed of two or more words combined into one item. It may be two nouns, an adjective and a noun, a verb and a noun, or an adverb and a verb.

canopy bed (noun and noun)
bluebird (noun and adjective)
starting pistol (verb and noun)
downfall (adverb and verb)

Nouns may be described as either concrete or abstract. A concrete noun is a person, place, or thing which can be perceived with the physical senses. An abstract noun is an idea, quality, condition, or activity. Abstract nouns are usually singular.

portrait (concrete) antiquity (abstract)
song (concrete) harmony (abstract)
statement (concrete) ignorance (abstract)

Pronoun

A pronoun takes the place of a noun.

The personal pronouns are pronouns that refer to the speaker, the person being spoken to, or the person being spoken about. The personal pronouns come in three cases: nominative [*I, you* (singular), *he, she, it, we, you* (plural), *they*] (which are used as subjects and predicate nominatives), objective (*me, you, him, her, it, us, you, them*) (which are used, primarily, as direct objects, indirect objects, and objects of prepositions), and possessive [*my, mine, your* (singular), *yours* (singular), *his, her, hers, its, our, ours, your* (plural), *yours* (plural), *their, theirs*] (which, in effect, are pronouns used as adjectives indicating possession).

What varieties of livestock did the English colonists bring with *them* in the seventeenth century?
By *his* works on the so-called "metaphysical poets" of the seventeenth century, Eliot was able to renew interest in such poets as Donne and Herbert.

The personal pronouns, when combined with *–self* or *–selves*, may be used reflexively (to refer to the subject) or intensively (to emphasize).

Did Ophelia kill *herself*? (reflexive)
The settler built *himself* a cabin in the valley. (reflexive)

Hamlet *himself* addressed the ghost. (intensive)
I was struck by the beauty of the house *itself*. (intensive)

Relative pronouns (*who, whom, whose, which, that, what,* etc.) are used to begin certain dependent clauses.

Never send to know [for *whom* the bell tolls]; it tolls for thee. –John Donne
We have left undone those things [*which* we ought to have done]; and we have done those things [*which* we ought not to have done].
–Book of Common Prayer

Interrogative pronouns (*who, whom, whose, which, what*) are used to ask questions.

In *what* year was the Parthenon built?

Whose woods are these?

Demonstrative pronouns (*this, these, that, those*) are used to point out the person or thing being referred to.

These are the times that try men's souls. –Thomas Paine
Recently, *those* quilts were shown in various art exhibitions.

Indefinite pronouns (*each, either, neither, one, anybody, anyone, everybody, everyone, nobody, no one, somebody, someone, both, few, several, many, some, any, none, all, most*) are quite general and unspecific in their reference.

Something there is that doesn't love a wall. –Robert Frost
Most of the change we think we see in life is due to truths' being in or out of favor. –Robert Frost

Adjective

An adjective describes or modifies a noun or pronoun. Adjectives generally answer the questions "which one," "what kind," "how many," or "whose."

I have seen the *eternal* Footman hold my coat, and snicker. –T. S. Eliot
A flock of *thirty-eight* wild turkeys were grazing in the meadow.

An adjective frequently goes directly in front of the word it is modifying, though occasionally it is placed immediately after the noun.

This is the forest *primeval*. –Henry Wadsworth Longfellow

Adjectives also may follow linking verbs and describe the subject (a predicate adjective).

Have mercy upon me, O Lord, for I am *weak*. –Psalm 6:2

Adverb

An adverb describes or modifies a verb, adjective, or another adverb. Adverbs generally answer such questions as "how," "when," "where," "why," "how often," "to what extent," or "under what conditions."

He stood and walked *slowly* to the dais.
I believe that we shall arrive *Tuesday*.

An adverb usually goes directly before or after the word it is modifying, though occasionally it may be placed elsewhere (frequently at the beginning or end of the sentence).

Suddenly, the entire structure collapsed.
We shall discuss this matter in great detail *later*.

Preposition

A preposition shows the relation between the noun or pronoun coming after it (the object of the preposition) to some other word in the sentence. A preposition will thus always introduce a prepositional phrase. Prepositional phrases may be used as adjectives (modifying nouns or pronouns) or as adverbs (modifying verbs, adjectives, or adverbs).

Farewell, thou child [*of* my right hand], and joy. –Ben Jonson
Haply I think [*on* thee]. – William Shakespeare, "Sonnet 29"

Some words which are often used as prepositions may also be used (without objects) as adverbs.

We traveled *through* the woods. (preposition)
Do you think that we can get *through*? (adverb)

Conjunction

A conjunction joins words or groups of words.
Coordinating conjunctions (*and, but, or, nor, for, yet, so*) join items of equal value.

The memory of the just is blessed, *but* the name of the wicked shall rot.
–Proverbs 10:7
Grace be to you *and* peace, from God our Father *and* from the Lord Jesus Christ.
–Ephesians 1:2

Correlative conjunctions (*both ... and, not only ... but also, either ... or, neither ... nor*) are always used in pairs. They too join items of equal value.

The students need *not only* instruction in grammar *but also* practice in usage.

Thou art *neither* cold *nor* hot. –Revelation 3:15

Subordinating conjunctions (*after, although, because, since, until, while,* etc.) are used to introduce adverb clauses.

[*When* vice prevails, and impious men bear sway], the post of honour is a private station. –Joseph Addison
I immediately telephoned him [*after* I returned home].

Interjection

An interjection expresses an exclamation (either mild or strong) but is not grammatically connected to the rest of the sentence.

Alas, my lord, I beseech thee, lay not the sin upon us. –Numbers 12:11
No, that is not the correct answer.

Note that the part of speech of a word depends entirely upon its use in the sentence. The same word may be used as various parts of speech in different sentences.

The chairs were arranged in a *square*. (noun)
They constructed a *square* pedestal for the statue. (adjective)
He *squared* the hole using a sharp chisel. (verb)

Chapter 3
Syntax

The Sentence

A sentence is a group of words that expresses a complete thought and can stand alone. It begins with a capital letter and ends with an end mark (usually a period or a question mark, but sometimes an exclamation point). Sir Winston Churchill, the great British statesman, describes his education at Harrow, where his teacher taught sentence parsing or sentence analysis. Churchill says of his English teacher Mr. Somervell: "He taught it as no one else has ever taught it. Not only did we learn English parsing thoroughly, but we also practised continually English analysis. ... I learned it thoroughly. Thus I got into my bones the essential structure of the ordinary British sentence—which is a noble thing."[1] It is exactly that traditional method of sentence analysis that this book will instruct you in.

Syntax is the precise term for sentence analysis. It comes from two Greek words, *syn* meaning "together" and *tassein* meaning "to arrange." Hence, syntax is the way in which words are arranged or put together. In a highly inflected language, like Greek or Latin, the role of a particular word is usually identified by its ending.

Examine these forms for the Latin noun *lapis* (stone):

	singular	plural
subject or predicate nominative	lapis	lapidēs
possessive	lapidis	lapidum
indirect object	lapidī	lapidibus
direct object	lapidem	lapidēs
object of a preposition	lapide	lapidibus

[1] Winston Churchill, *My Early Life, A Roving Commission* (NY: Charles Seribner's Sons, 1958), 17.

The same method was employed in the various Germanic languages as well. The language of the ancient Germanic inhabitants of Britain (the Angles, Saxons, Jutes, and Frisians—nowadays frequently called simply the Anglo-Saxons) was, like the other Germanic languages, highly inflected as well.

Examine these forms of the Old English noun *stān* (stone):

	singular	plural
subject or predicate nominative	stān	stānas
possessive	stānes	stāna
indirect object or object of a preposition	stāne	stānum
direct object	stān	stānas

Now contrast those with these forms of the Modern English noun *stone*:

	singular	plural
possessive	stone's	stones'
all other forms	stone	stones

The good thing about indicating syntactical relationships by means of an inflection (addition of an ending or another change of spelling) was that it allowed a great amount of flexibility in sentence construction. When one saw the word *stānes*, one knew that it was used to show possession (stone's), regardless of where it was located in a sentence. As time passed, however, Old English became progressively simpler. Gradually almost all endings were abandoned. In addition to the modern form *stone*, there are only three other forms: *stone's* (to indicate possession), *stones* (to indicate plural), and *stones'* (to indicate plural possession).

As English developed from Old English to Middle English (in the 1100s or so) to Modern English (in the 1500s), the number of inflectional forms dropped from six to four (and those were retained only to show plural and possession). The same form of the noun would be used for a subject, a predicate nominative, an indirect object, a direct object, or the object of a preposition. To make up for this simplification of inflectional endings, however, there had to be an increased emphasis on word order; otherwise, the sentence would become incomprehensible. In Old English, the location of a noun in a sentence was not extremely important; the important thing was the ending. However, as the endings gradually were simplified, the location of the word in the sentence became very important. There is a great deal of difference between

The hunter killed the bear.

and

The bear killed the hunter.

As English developed, word order became very important for the understanding of syntax.

Locating the Verb and the Subject

The first thing to look for in a sentence is a verb. A verb is a word that expresses action (an action verb) or that is used to join the subject to the rest of the predicate (a linking verb). The subject is the noun or pronoun that answers the question "who" or "what" before the verb. The predicate is simply the verb (either action or linking) and the rest of the sentence. The verb may consist of merely one word, or it may consist of a main verb along with other helping or auxiliary verbs.

All verbs may be divided into two types: action and linking. An action verb may express physical, mental, or emotional action. A linking verb links the subject with the statement being made about the subject. Often (though not always) action and linking verbs are followed by complements. A complement is a word that is used to complete the meaning of the sentence, hence its name.

So far, we have identified three steps in the analysis of a sentence. First, find the verb. Then (by asking "who" or "what" before the verb), find the subject. Third, go back to the verb and decide whether it is an action verb or a linking verb. If it is an action verb, you will look for certain complements; if it is a linking verb, you will look for other complements (though a verb may not have any complement at all). Action verbs should be fairly easy to identify since they show some type of action. Linking verbs may be either forms of the verb *be* (such as *am, is, are, was, were, be, being, been*) or forms of verbs which in other situations might be action verbs. For instance, consider this sentence: *The children tasted the sauerkraut only tentatively.* The verb *tasted* is an action verb, showing what the subject (*children*) did. Now consider another sentence: *The sauerkraut tasted surprisingly good to them.* In this sentence the verb *tasted* is not an action verb at all; it does not show what the subject (*sauerkraut*) did; rather it links the subject (*sauerkraut*) with the complement (*good*). These action verbs which can also be used as linking verbs might be called "sometimes action/sometimes linking" verbs. The most common verbs of this type are *taste, feel, smell, seem, grow, remain, stay, appear, become, look, sound*.

A verb along with its helping verbs may be referred to as a verb phrase. Sometimes this verb phrase may be interrupted by some other word (such as an adverb). Take care to find the main verb and any helping verbs that go along with it.

The dosage *has been* gradually *diminished.*
The patient's condition *was* not *improving* at all.

Some English sentences will present some added difficulty in locating the subject. Consider these four sentences.

Were they mindful of the consequences of their actions?
This is an interrogative sentence (a question). Questions frequently begin with the verb (or a helping verb) rather than the subject. The subject of the verb *were* is *they*.

There are over a hundred poems in the collection.
There and *here* are not nouns or pronouns and hence cannot be subjects. When they are used to begin a sentence, the subject is frequently after the verb. The subject of the verb *are* is *poems*.

Put the books in their proper places on the shelf.
This is an imperative sentence (a command or request). Such sentences have the pronoun *you* as their subjects but frequently omit the *you*. We say that the subject is "*you* understood." We understand that *you* (either singular or plural) is the subject, even though it is not actually written.

Around the cornice of the Tudor room was carved a passage from the Psalter.
Sometimes sentences begin with prepositional phrases. The subject of a sentence is never in a prepositional phrase. In such cases the subject may be located after the verb. The subject of the verb *was carved* is *passage*.

In such sentences as these it will be easier to find the subject if you first turn them into sentences with more normal word order.

They were mindful of the consequences of their actions. (*They* is the subject)
Over a hundred sonnets are in the collection. (*sonnets* is the subject)
You put the books in their proper places on the shelf. (*You* is the subject)
A passage from the Psalter was carved around the cornice of the Tudor room. (*passage* is the subject)

Locating Complements after Linking Verbs

Although some sentences are quite complete with only a subject and a verb, many sentences need to be completed by some additional element. Many sentences require complements to complete the meaning of the subject and verb. Clearly, the term *complement* comes from the same source as the verb *to complete*; a complement completes the meaning of the sentence. Certain complements come after linking verbs, and other complements come after action verbs.

Predicate Nominative

If the verb is a linking verb, it may be followed by a predicate nominative. The predicate nominative is a noun or pronoun which usually follows the verb and renames the subject. Many terms of English grammar (such as *predicate nominative*) may seem difficult. Frequently, these terms are quite old. When English grammar was first described in the Middle Ages, the terms used for it were often borrowed from Latin grammar. For instance, *predicate* comes from the Latin word *praedicare*, meaning "to declare" or "to say." The predicate says something about the subject. The term *nominative* comes from the Latin word *nomen*, meaning "a name"; it is simply a Latinate form of our English word *noun*. Hence, a predicate nominative is a noun or pronoun which comes after a linking verb (either a "be" verb or one of the "sometimes action/sometimes linking" verbs) and renames the subject.

Rebellion to tyrants is obedience to God. (*obedience* is the predicate nominative)
Even after the corporate merger, Davis remained the chief executive officer. (*chief executive officer* is the predicate nominative)

Predicate Adjective

A linking verb may also be followed by an adjective which describes the subject. Such a complement is simply called a predicate adjective.

The march of the human mind is slow. –Edmund Burke (*slow* is the predicate adjective)
I felt singularly unwell the rest of the day. (*unwell* is the predicate adjective)

Locating Complements after Action Verbs

Direct Object

Predicate nominatives and predicate adjectives will be used only with linking verbs; they will never be used with action verbs. The primary complement used with an action verb is a direct object. A direct object is a noun or pronoun which usually comes after an action verb and which receives the action of the verb. It will answer the questions "whom" or "what" after the verb.

Elizabeth Bennet and Mr. Darcy took an immediate dislike to one another.

The verb is *took*. The compound subject is *Elizabeth Bennet and Mr. Darcy*. The verb *took* is an action verb. *Elizabeth Bennet and Mr. Darcy took* what? They took *an immediate dislike*. The noun *dislike* is the direct object. A direct object, being a noun, may be modified or described by adjectives such as *an* and *immediate*. Verbs that take direct objects are called "transitive" verbs, from the Latin verb *transire*, meaning "to go across."

Not all action verbs have direct objects. Some verbs by their very nature do not take direct objects. These verbs are called "intransitive" ("not transitive"). Such a verb is an action verb, but there is no noun or pronoun that the action "goes across" to.

The deer fled. (*fled* is an action verb, but it is an intransitive verb and needs no direct object)

Indirect Object

If a sentence has an action verb and a direct object, it may also have an indirect object. An indirect object will meet three criteria: it will be a noun or pronoun, it will answer the questions "to whom" or "for whom" (or "to what" or "for what"), and it will be located between the action verb and direct object.

The situation offered Cicero a political opportunity.

The verb is *offered*, and the subject is *situation*. *Offered* is a transitive action verb. *The situation offered* what? It offered an *opportunity*. You may be tempted to think that *Cicero* is the direct object, but obviously the situation did not offer *Cicero*, it offered an *opportunity*. *Cicero* is the indirect object. It is a noun, it answers the question "to whom," and it is located between the action verb and the direct object. English has another way of expressing the same idea. We can say, "The situation offered a political opportunity to Cicero." While this means the very same thing, *Cicero* is not now an indirect object, but is part of a prepositional phrase. Verbs, subjects, and complements are never located in prepositional phrases. While these two sentences mean practically the same thing, they are not constructed grammatically the same way. Sentence analysis is the process of analyzing how a sentence is constructed grammatically.

Objective Complement

If a sentence has a direct object, it may also have an objective complement. An objective complement is a noun, pronoun, or adjective which comes after a direct object and renames or describes that direct object. (A sentence cannot have an objective complement unless it has a direct object, and a sentence cannot have a direct object unless it has an action verb.) You may notice that a sentence with an objective complement frequently has a verb that indicates a change of some type in the direct object.

The Senate elected Cicero consul.

The verb is *elected*, and the subject is *the Senate*. *Elected* is an action verb. *The Senate elected* whom? It elected *Cicero*, so *Cicero* is the direct object. *Consul* is the objective complement. It is a noun and renames the direct object *Cicero*.

The first owners of the house painted the parlor green.

The verb is *painted*, and the subject is *owners*. *Painted* is an action verb. *The first owners painted* what? They painted *the parlor*, so *parlor* is the direct object. *Green* is the objective complement. It is an adjective and describes the direct object *parlor*.

Notice that sentences with direct and indirect objects are quite different from sentences with direct objects and objective complements. Do not get these confused. Again, these are two different sentence patterns. They might be described this way: S AV IO DO and S AV DO OC. If you follow the sentence analysis method described in this book, you should be able to tell the difference between these two sentence patterns. Consider this sentence:

Jefferson named his home near Charlottesville Monticello.

The verb is *named*, and the subject is *Jefferson*. *Jefferson named* whom or what? You may be tempted to think that *Monticello* is the direct object and that therefore *home* is the indirect object. But does *home* answer the questions "to what" or "for what"? *Jefferson named Monticello to his home? Jefferson named Monticello for his home?* No, Jefferson did not name *Monticello*, he named *his home*. Notice that the verb *named* indicates some change to its object. Jefferson named his home *Monticello*.

Retained Object

Earlier, it was noted that some verbs are intransitive verbs. Such verbs do not take direct objects. Verbs that do take direct objects are said to be transitive verbs. The action "goes across" from the subject to the direct object. Both transitive verbs and intransitive verbs are action verbs. Both types of verbs show action of some type. Intransitive verbs simply do not require anything to complete their action: they need no complement. Transitive verbs do require something to complete their action. When a transitive verb has a direct object, that verb is said to be transitive active. The subject is actively doing something to the direct object.

Izaak Walton wrote a book on fishing.

The verb is *wrote*, and the subject is *Izaak Walton*. *Izaak Walton wrote* what? He wrote *a book*. *Wrote* is an action verb, and *book* is the direct object. Hence, *wrote* is a transitive active action verb.

But this same sentence could be restructured. Take *book* (the direct object) and make it into the subject. Take *Izaak Walton* and make it into a prepositional phrase using the preposition *by*. *A book on fishing ... by Izaak Walton*. Now turn the verb *wrote* (a transitive active action verb) into a transitive passive action verb. Use the form of the verb that ends in *ed* or *en* (or its equivalent) and use a form of the verb *to be* as its helping verb. In other words, turn *wrote* into *was written*. So the sentence *Izaak Walton wrote a book on fishing* becomes *A book on fishing was written by Izaak Walton*. If this new sentence seems somewhat weak and less than totally effective, it is because the verb is passive rather than active. Generally, we use transitive passive action verbs only when we wish to indicate this weakness or passivity for some reason. [See the further discussion on passive voice in Chapter 4, "The Verb and Its Usage."]

Consider another sentence:

The judges gave the winner of the race a crown of laurel.

The verb is *gave*, and the subject is *the judges*. *The judges gave* what? The judges gave *a crown*. *Gave* is an action verb, and *crown* is the direct object. Hence, *gave* is a transitive active action verb. Also notice that *the winner*, located between the action verb and the direct object, is an indirect object.

Now restructure this sentence, making the verb passive. First, take the direct object (*crown*) and make it the subject. Then take the subject (*the judges*) and make it into a prepositional phrase using the preposition *by*. *A crown of laurel ... by the judges*. Now turn the verb *gave* (a transitive active action verb) into a transitive passive action verb. Use the past participle (the form of the verb that ends in *ed* or *en* or its equivalent) and a form of the verb *to be* as a helping verb. So the sentence will become *A crown of laurel was given the winner of the race by the judges.* Notice that everything changed except for one thing. The direct object became the subject in the new sentence. The subject became a prepositional phrase in the new sentence. The transitive active action verb became a transitive passive action verb in the new sentence. The only thing that was kept or retained in its previous position was the noun *the winner*. In the first sentence *the winner* was the indirect object. But *the winner* cannot be called the indirect object in the second sentence, since it technically has no direct object. Since we kept or retained this word from the previous sentence, we call it the retained object.

You could also have turned the indirect object *winner* into the subject. Then the sentence would have become *The winner of the race was given a crown of laurel by the judges.* This is probably the much more common way of using the passive voice. *The winner* would have turned from indirect object to subject. *The judges* would have turned from subject to prepositional phrase. The transitive active action verb *gave* would have become the transitive passive action verb *was given*. The only thing retained in its previous position would be the noun *crown*. In the new sentence *crown* would be called the retained object.

Sentence Patterns

There are basically eight patterns followed by English sentences.

S AV	We laughed loudly.
S AV DO	Washington defeated Cornwallis at Yorktown.
S AV IO DO	I sent my friends postcards from France.
S AV DO OC	The president appointed him ambassador to Greece.
S AV RO	Alice was given a watch by her boyfriend.
S LV	He is.
S LV PN	They are cousins.
S LV PA	The baby is sick.

Phrases

A phrase is a group of words used together as one part of speech. For instance, a phrase might be used as an adjective or an adverb or a noun. Unlike a clause, a phrase does not have a subject and a verb.

Prepositional Phrase

A prepositional phrase consists of a preposition and its object (a noun or pronoun) and any modifiers of the object. (The object of the preposition may be compound.) The preposition shows the relationship between the noun or pronoun (the object of the preposition) and some other word in the sentence (the word that the prepositional phrase is modifying). Become familiar with the most common prepositions.

aboard	among	between	from	over	underneath
about	around	beyond	in	past	until
above	at	but	into	since	unto
across	before	by	like	through	up
after	behind	down	near	throughout	upon
against	below	during	of	to	with
along	beneath	except	off	toward	within
amid	beside	for	on	under	without

A few prepositions consist of more than one word. Do not think of them as separate words but as one preposition.

according to	because of	in front of	instead of	out of
as for	except for	in spite of	on account of	regardless of

A prepositional phrase may be used as either an adjective or adverb. Like an adjective, it can modify a noun or pronoun. Like an adverb, it can modify a verb, an adjective, or an adverb.

There is no royal road (to geometry). –Euclid (used as an adjective—modifying the noun *road*)
Everyone (at the press conference) was shocked by the announcement. (used as an adjective—modifying the pronoun *Everyone*)
Never find your delight (in another's misfortune). –Publius Syrus (used as an adverb—modifying the verb *find*)
The general was furious (about the outcome). (used as an adverb—modifying the adjective *furious*)
They returned later (in the afternoon). (used as an adverb—modifying the adverb *later*)

A prepositional phrase located at the beginning of a sentence (and possibly followed by a comma) is probably used as an adverb modifying the verb.

(After his long absence,) Ulysses returned to his home in Ithaca. (used as an adverb—modifying the verb *returned*)

A prepositional phrase located at the beginning of a sentence right before a verb is probably used as an adverb modifying that verb.

(In my Father's house) are many mansions. –John 14:2 (used as an adverb—modifying the verb *are*)

Verbal Phrase

Every verb in English has various forms. The verb *write*, for instance, has such forms as *write, writes, wrote, will write, has written, had written, will have written*, etc. Of all these numerous verb forms, four have traditionally been called the four principal (or primary) parts. These are the main forms that all of the many different verb forms are made of. The four principal parts are called the present, present participle, past, and past participle. The present participle is the present form plus *ing*. The past and past participle are often made by adding *ed* (or *d* or *t* or *en*) to the present part.

There are, of course, many irregular verbs in English. Become familiar with the four principal parts of the most common irregular verbs.

present	**present participle**	**past**	**past participle**
beat	beating	beat	beaten
begin	beginning	began	begun
bite	biting	bit	bitten
blow	blowing	blew	blown
break	breaking	broke	broken
bring	bringing	brought	brought
build	building	built	built
burst	bursting	burst	burst
buy	buying	bought	bought
choose	choosing	chose	chosen
come	coming	came	come
do	doing	did	done
draw	drawing	drew	drawn
drink	drinking	drank	drunk
eat	eating	ate	eaten
fall	falling	fell	fallen
fly	flying	flew	flown
freeze	freezing	froze	frozen
get	getting	got	got/gotten
give	giving	gave	given
go	going	went	gone
grow	growing	grew	grown
hold	holding	held	held
know	knowing	knew	known
lay	laying	laid	laid
lead	leading	led	led
leave	leaving	left	left

lie	lying	lay	lain
lose	losing	lost	lost
pay	paying	paid	paid
ride	riding	rode	ridden
ring	ringing	rang	rung
rise	rising	rose	risen
run	running	ran	run
say	saying	said	said
see	seeing	saw	seen
set	setting	set	set
shake	shaking	shook	shaken
show	showing	showed	shown
shrink	shrinking	shrank	shrunk
sing	singing	sang	sung
sink	sinking	sank	sunk
sit	sitting	sat	sat
speak	speaking	spoke	spoken
spring	springing	sprang	sprung
steal	stealing	stole	stolen
swear	swearing	swore	sworn
swim	swimming	swam	swum
take	taking	took	taken
tear	tearing	tore	torn
think	thinking	thought	thought
throw	throwing	threw	thrown
wear	wearing	wore	worn
weep	weeping	wept	wept
win	winning	won	won
write	writing	wrote	written

The many different verb forms may certainly be used merely as verbs. Sometimes, however, some of the verb forms are used as some other part of speech, as an adjective, a noun, or perhaps as an adverb. When a verb form is used as some part of speech other than a verb it is called a verbal ("verb-like").

Participial Phrase

The second principal part (the present participle) and the fourth principal part (the past participle) may be used as adjectives, modifying nouns or pronouns. However, they retain some of the properties of verbs: for instance, they can be modified by adverbs (or adverb prepositional phrases) and can have noun or pronoun objects. (Such objects would be called direct objects if the verb form were being used as a verb; when the verb form is used as a verbal, the noun or pronoun object is usually simply referred to as the object of the verbal.) The participial phrase consists of the participle, its object (if it has one), and its modifiers (if it has any). Though the phrase consists of more than one word, think of the phrase altogether as one part of speech. The participial phrase is used as an adjective, modifying a noun or pronoun.

> The (*bubbling*) brook refreshed the weary travelers. (The participial phrase consists of just the participle.)
>
> The man (*building* the stone wall) is my Uncle Rob. (The participial phrase consists of the participle and its object.)
>
> We heard of another manuscript (recently *discovered* in the Middle East). (The participial phrase consists of the participle and its adverbial modifier *recently* and the adverb prepositional phrase *in the Middle East*.)
>
> Congress shall make no law (*respecting* an establishment of religion) or (*prohibiting* the free exercise thereof). –First Amendment, U.S. Constitution (One participial phrase consists of the participle and its object and a prepositional phrase modifying that object. The other consists of the participle plus its object. Notice that this participial phrase is compound.)

Participles exist in English in only two tenses: present and past. Hence, there are four participles in English: present tense active voice (or present active), present tense passive voice (or present passive), past tense active voice (or perfect active), and past tense passive voice (or perfect passive).[2] Examine this chart:

present tense active voice	**present tense passive voice**
loving	loved / being loved[3]
going	–
being	–
past tense active voice	**past tense passive voice**
having loved	loved / having been loved[4]
having gone	–
having been	–

[2] The word *perfect* comes from the Latin word *perfectus* and simply means "finished" or "completed." In grammatical nomenclature it frequently is used in place of the word *past*.

[3] "Being loved" is the progressive form of the present tense and indicates continuous action in the present.

[4] "Having been loved" is the progressive form of the past tense and indicates continuous action in the past.

Linking verbs and intransitive action verbs by their very nature cannot be passive and thus have no passive participial forms.

Notice how the four different participles are formed:

–the present tense active voice is formed by using the "present participle" alone (*loving*)
–the present tense passive voice is formed by using the "past participle" alone (*loved*) or by using the "past participle" with the auxiliary verb form *being* in front of it (*being loved*)
–the past tense active voice is formed by using the "past participle" with the auxiliary verb form *having* in front of it (*having loved*)
–the past tense passive voice is formed by using the "past participle" alone (*loved*) or by using the "past participle" with the auxiliary verb form *having been* in front of it (*having been loved*)

Examine these participial phrases and note the different tenses (present tense and past tense) and voices (active voice and passive voice) used.

The course (*giving* me the most trouble) is calculus. (transitive active action verb—present tense)
Our honoree is a woman (*respected* by all). (transitive passive action verb—present tense)
The letters (*being sent* to all the applicants) contain a schedule of the courses. (transitive passive action verb—present tense)
The flowers (*growing* on the hillside) are rhododendrons. (intransitive action verb—present tense)
(*Being* a citizen,) you have certain responsibilities to the state. (linking verb—present tense)
(*Feeling* unwell), I am going home. (linking verb—present tense)
(*Having finished* our chores), we sat down for a well-earned rest. (transitive active action verb—past tense)
The men (*killed* at the Battle of Gettysburg) numbered over fifty thousand. (transitive passive action verb—past tense)
The young buds of the fruit trees, (*having been frozen* by the low temperatures), soon withered. (transitive passive action verb—past tense)
The old clock, (*having stood* in that hall for three hundred years), remained a silent witness of the family's former prosperity. (intransitive action verb—past tense)
(Not *having been* present in class the day before), the student was unprepared for the test. (linking verb—past tense)
(*Having grown* weary of his excuses), the boss fired him. (linking verb—past tense)

Gerund Phrase

The second principal part (the present participle) may also be used as a noun. (The past participle may not.) This verb form ending in *ing* and used as a noun is called a gerund. Like participles, gerunds may also have objects and modifiers. The gerund phrase consists of the gerund and its objects and modifiers (if any). The entire gerund phrase acts like one noun and can therefore be anything a noun can be. The gerund phrase is used most commonly as the subject, the predicate nominative, the direct object, and the object of a preposition. Remember, however, that a gerund can be used any way a noun can be.

(*Gardening*) gives me many hours of pleasure. (used as the subject)
His favorite pastime is (*gardening*). (used as the predicate nominative)
My grandfather greatly enjoys (*gardening*). (used as the direct object)
Mr. Edkins keeps fit by (*gardening*). (used as the object of the preposition *by*)
(*Playing* the organ) requires both musical ability and physical coordination. (used as the subject)
Dr. Picirilli's hobby is (*collecting* rare and unusual stamps). (used as the predicate nominative)
Did you finish (*reading* all of Tolkien's works)? (used as the direct object)
I asked Ralph for information about (*grafting* apple trees). (used as the object of the preposition *about*)

Like participles, gerunds too come in four forms: present tense active voice (or present active), present tense passive voice (or present passive), past tense active voice (or perfect active), and past tense passive voice (or perfect passive). Examine this chart:

present tense active voice	**present tense passive voice**
loving	being loved
going	–
being	–

past tense active voice	**past tense passive voice**
having loved	having been loved
having gone	–
having been	–

Notice that the gerund (unlike the participle) never uses the "past participle" alone.

Examine these gerund phrases and note the different tenses (present tense and past tense) and voices (active voice and passive voice) used.

He enjoys (*playing* old ballads on the fiddle). (transitive active action verb—present tense)
I certainly did not enjoy (*being passed* over for the promotion). (transitive passive action verb—present tense)
We appreciate your (*coming* along with us today). (intransitive action verb—present tense)
(*Being* the oldest child in the family) sometimes brings with it certain unwanted responsibilities. (linking verb—present tense)
By (*remaining* silent), even a fool can be considered wise. (linking verb—present tense)
His (*having* already *told* her about our conversation) caused certain difficulties. (transitive active action verb—past tense)
Princess Mary obviously disapproved of her mother's (*having been divorced* by Henry VIII). (transitive passive action verb—past tense)
I was not aware of his (*having* already *arrived*). (intransitive action verb—past tense)
The children were never aware of their father's (*having been* a soldier). (linking verb—past tense)
My old friend's (*having become* my boss) necessitated tact and delicacy on both our parts. (linking verb—past tense)

Since gerund phrases are nouns, they must frequently be preceded by a possessive noun or pronoun.

We appreciate *your* (not *you*) *visiting* us today.
I was impressed by my old *professor's* (not *professor*) *remembering* me after all those years.

Infinitive Phrase

The infinitive is the first principal part with the word *to* in front of it. Like participles and gerunds, infinitives may also have objects and modifiers. The infinitive phrase consists of the infinitive and its objects and modifiers (if any). Like a participial phrase, the infinitive phrase can be used as an adjective, modifying a noun or pronoun. Like a gerund phrase, the infinitive phrase can be used as a noun. While the infinitive phrase (like the gerund phrase) can do anything a noun can do, it is used most commonly as the subject, the predicate nominative, the direct object, and the object of a preposition. The infinitive phrase can also be used as an adverb, modifying verbs, adjectives, or adverbs. An infinitive phrase located at the beginning of a sentence and followed by a comma is usually used as an adverb modifying the verb.

The cows (*to be milked*) were driven into the barn. (used as an adjective modifying the noun *cows*)

(*To make* anything of beauty) requires both creativity and hard work. (used as a noun—as the subject)
Helen's goal was (*to complete* her degree in chemistry). (used as a noun—as the predicate nominative)
We wanted (*to get* the hay in before the rain). (used as a noun—as the direct object)
The boys did everything except (*mow* the back yard). (used as a noun—as the object of the preposition *except*)
[Notice that when an infinitive is used as the object of a preposition it is common to omit the *to* from the infinitive.]

(*To examine* books in the archives), first consult the librarian. (used as an adverb modifying the verb *consult*)
We were certainly unhappy (*to hear* about the recent Supreme Court decision). (used as an adverb modifying the adjective *unhappy*)
Unfortunately, he did not study hard enough (*to pass* the course). (used as an adverb modifying the adverb *enough*)

Unlike participles and gerunds, the infinitive can sometimes take a subject. [For a discussion of the case of a pronoun used as the subject of an infinitive see chapter 5.]

My parents wanted (me *to spend* more time on my studies). (*me* is the subject of the infinitive *to spend*)

Like participles and gerunds, infinitives also come in four forms: present tense active voice (or present active), present tense passive voice (or present passive), past tense active voice (or perfect active), and past tense passive voice (or perfect passive). Examine this chart:

present tense active voice	**present tense passive voice**
to love	to be loved
to go	–
to be	–
past tense active voice	**past tense passive voice**
to have loved	to have been loved
to have gone	–
to have been	–

Examine these infinitive phrases and note the different tenses (present tense and past tense) and voices (active voice and passive voice) used.

It is a foolish thing (*to make* a long prologue and to be short in the story itself). –2 Maccabees 2:25 (transitive active action verb—present tense)
Make them (*to be numbered* with thy saints, in glory everlasting). –Book of Common Prayer (transitive passive action verb—present tense)
It is a fearful thing (*to fall* into the hands of the living God). –Hebrews 10:31 (intransitive action verb—present tense)
Though he with giants fight, he will make good his right (*to be* a pilgrim). –John Bunyan (linking verb—present tense)
He sought (*to grow* rich, by any means). (linking verb—present tense)
She was glad (*to have brought* up such children). (transitive active action verb—past tense)
It is good (*to have been taught* hard work in one's youth). (transitive passive action verb—past tense)
The pavement seems (*to have ended*). (intransitive action verb—past tense)
I am happy (*to have been* of some help to you). (linking verb—past tense)
He was not entirely unhappy (*to have remained* an old bachelor). (linking verb—past tense)

Infinitive phrases are also used to complete the meaning of certain verbs, such as *ought, decide, want, desire, need*, etc. These are sometimes referred to as complementary infinitives.

This construction project ought (to have been completed by now).

They can also be used for indirect statements, commands, or questions.

My father told me, "Wash the upstairs windows." (direct command)
My father told me (to wash the upstairs windows). (indirect command)

Appositive Phrase

The words *opposite* and *apposite* are opposites. While things that are in opposition are in disagreement with one another, things that are in apposition are in agreement. An appositive is a noun or pronoun that usually follows another noun or pronoun and renames or identifies it. That appositive together with any adjectives modifying it forms an appositive phrase.

John Eliot, (a Puritan *minister* of the seventeenth century), translated the Bible into the language of the Pequot Indian nation. (appositive of *John Eliot*)

My brother (*Samuel*) practices law in Berea, Kentucky. (appositive of *brother*)

You will note that some appositive phrases are set off with commas and some are not. Put commas around appositive phrases which are nonessential. If you can leave the appositive out without doing any damage to the sense of the sentence it is nonessential and should be set off with commas. If it is essential, do not set it off with commas. Note this distinction in the two sentences above.

It is not uncommon for a gerund or infinitive (or, as we shall see later, a noun clause) to be used as an appositive.

Columbus's goal, (to reach the Indies by sailing west across the Atlantic), proved illusory. (renames the noun *goal*)

Do not confuse appositives, which may rename or identify any noun in a sentence, either with a predicate nominative, which accompanies a linking verb and renames only the subject, or an objective complement, which follows a direct object and indicates some change in that direct object.

Mr. Kurtz's "Intended" is a pale English woman clothed in black. (the noun *woman* is the predicate nominative, renaming the subject *"Intended"*)

Marlow never gives the young lady's name but always calls her "Kurtz's 'Intended.'" (*Kurtz's 'Intended'* is the objective complement renaming the direct object *her* and indicating some change in *her*)

At the end of the novel, Marlow meets Mr. Kurtz's "Intended," a pale English woman clothed in black. (the noun *woman* is an appositive, renaming or identifying the direct object *"Intended"*)

Consider this sentence: *It is not uncommon to use an appositive in this way.* In such a sentence the pronoun *it*—though technically the subject of the verb *is*—is used basically as an expletive, starting a formulaic sentence, not unlike the use of *here* and *there*. Frequently the sentence ends with a gerund phrase, an infinitive phrase (or, as we shall see, a noun clause) as an appositive, identifying the subject *it*.

It is not wise (to think too highly of yourself).

Nominative Absolute

The Latin adjective *absolutus* means "set free" or "unattached." An absolute phrase is so called because it has no grammatical connection with the rest of the sentence. A nominative absolute consists of a noun (from the Latin *nomen*) or a pronoun (in the nominative case) followed by a participle or a participial phrase.

> *The temperature dropping rapidly*, I decided to bring in more wood for the fire.

Notice that the noun *temperature* is not grammatically connected with the rest of the sentence at all; it is neither the subject nor a complement nor an object in some other phrase. This is a nominative absolute.

> The barometric pressure, *dropping rapidly*, indicated a sudden change in weather.

Barometric pressure is grammatically connected with the rest of the sentence; it is the subject of the sentence. This is not a nominative absolute; *dropping rapidly* is simply a participial phrase modifying the subject.

Some nominatives absolute[5] are used so commonly that they have become clichés.

> *All things considered*, it was a pleasant holiday.

Clauses

Whereas a phrase is a group of words without a subject and a verb, a clause is a group of words with both a subject and a verb. There are two types of clauses: independent and dependent (or main and subordinate). An independent clause can stand alone as a complete sentence. A dependent or subordinate clause, however, cannot stand alone as a complete sentence; rather, it is used as a single part of speech, as an adjective, a noun, or an adverb.

> Corsica, [which lies in the Mediterranean Sea], has long been under French influence.

The clause *Corsica ... has long been under French influence* is independent and can stand alone as a complete sentence. However, the clause *which lies*

[5] The plural of *nominative absolute* should be *nominatives absolute*, since *nominative* is the noun being modified by the adjective *absolute*, similar to *mothers-in-law* and *attorneys general*. However, in recent years it has become common (*horribile dictu!*) to use *nominative absolutes* as the plural.

in the Mediterranean Sea is dependent and can not stand alone as a complete sentence.

Really, the use of a dependent clause with an independent clause is simply one way of joining together two sentences. Consider these two sentences:

> The prisoners were in the Soviet gulag.
> The prisoners suffered greatly.

These two sentences have in common the word *prisoners*. The two sentences can, in effect, be "spliced" together at that point. We replace the word *prisoners* with the relative *who* and turn the first sentence into an adjective clause modifying the word *prisoners*.

> The prisoners who were in the Soviet gulag suffered greatly.

We say that the word *prisoners* is the antecedent of the relative *who*. An antecedent is the noun or pronoun that a relative refers to. Notice that the antecedent of the relative and the noun or pronoun that the adjective clause is modifying are the same word.

Adjective Clause

An adjective clause is a dependent clause which modifies a noun or pronoun. Though it is a full clause, with its own individual verb, subject, complements, phrases, etc., nonetheless it functions as one single part of speech, an adjective modifying a noun or pronoun.

> The stone [*that the builders rejected*] has become the cornerstone.

> The dependent clause *that the builders rejected* serves as an adjective modifying *stone*.

Adjective clauses begin with words called relatives. Relatives show the relationship between the adjective clause and the noun or pronoun that the adjective clause is modifying. The most common relatives used to start adjective clauses are as follows: *who, whom, whose, which, that, when,* and *where*. The relative, in addition to showing the relationship of the clause to the noun or pronoun being modified, actually serves a grammatical function in the dependent clause. Within the dependent clause the relatives *who, whom, which,* and *that* will be pronouns and will serve as some type of substantive in the clause (subject, predicate nominative, direct object, indirect object, object of a preposition, etc.). *Whose* (and sometimes *which*) may serve as an adjective modifying a noun or pronoun. *When* and *where* will be adverbs modifying the verb of the dependent clause.

Do you know the girl [*who* owns this car]?
The verb in the adjective clause is *owns*.
The relative *who* is the subject of *owns*.
Car is the direct object.
The antecedent of *who* is the noun *girl*.
The adjective clause modifies the noun *girl*.

The watermelons [*which* we planted] did not come up.
The verb in the adjective clause is *planted*.
The subject of *planted* is *we*.
Which is the direct object.
The antecedent of *which* is the noun *watermelons*.
The adjective clause modifies the noun *watermelons*.

We did not know the family [*whose* house burned down].
The verb in the adjective clause is *burned*.
The subject of *burned* is *house*.
There are no complements in the adjective clause.
The relative *whose* is a possessive pronoun (in effect an adjective modifying the noun *house*).
The antecedent of *whose* is the noun *family*.
The adjective clause modifies the noun *family*.

Is Amanda the girl [*whom* he likes]?
The verb in the adjective clause is *likes*.
The subject of *likes* is *he*.
Whom is the direct object.
The antecedent of *whom* is the noun *girl*.
The adjective clause modifies the noun *girl*.

Notice that the adjective clause always begins with the relative, even if the relative is not the subject of the adjective clause. English begins the adjective clause with the relative in order to let the reader know the relationship of the clause to the noun being modified. There is only one exception to this rule. If the relative is used as the object of a preposition, you include the preposition within the adjective clause.

I do not know the name of the person [(to *whom*) I handed the envelope].
The verb in the adjective clause is *handed*.

The subject of *handed* is *I*.
Envelope is the direct object.
The relative *whom* is used as the object of the preposition *to*; therefore, we include the preposition within the adjective clause.
The antecedent of *whom* is the noun *person*.
The adjective clause modifies the noun *person*.

Notice that the relative, in addition to pointing out that an adjective clause is starting, actually serves some grammatical function within that adjective clause. It may be the subject of the adjective clause or the direct object or the object of a preposition. It may be used as an adjective (like *whose*). It may even be used as an adverb (like *when* and *where*).

Stratford Hall is the place [*where* Robert E. Lee was born].
The verb in the adjective clause is *was born*.
The subject of *was born* is *Robert E. Lee*.
The relative *where* is used as an adverb modifying the verb *was born*.
Where refers to the noun *place*.
The adjective clause modifies the noun *place*.

Do you know the year [*when* the Battle of Saratoga occurred]?
The verb in the adjective clause is *occurred*.
The subject of *occurred* is *the Battle of Saratoga*.
The relative *when* is used as an adverb modifying the verb *occurred*.
When refers to the noun *year*.
The adjective clause modifies the noun *year*.

Notice that in every case except one the relative is the very first word in the adjective clause. If the relative is used as the object of a preposition, it will be the second word in the adjective clause, right after the preposition itself.

Sometimes the relative is omitted from an adjective clause. Much like the "understood" *you* of a command or request, this relative is also "understood" to be present, though not expressed. It may help you to put in an appropriate relative in order to analyze the syntax of the clause correctly.

Have you seen the packages [I brought with me]?
The verb in the adjective clause is *brought*.
The subject of *brought* is *I*.
The relative to be used as the direct object is missing.

Add a relative such as *that* or *which*.
Have you seen the packages [*that* I brought with me]?

Noun Clause

A dependent clause can also be used as a noun. Much like a gerund phrase, a noun clause can be used in any way that a noun can be used: subject, predicate nominative, direct object, indirect object, objective complement, retained object, object of a preposition, or appositive. However, by far the most common uses of the noun clause are subject, predicate nominative, direct object, and object of a preposition.

[Whoever borrowed my dictionary] should return it. (used as the subject)
Will's hope is [that he can buy a small farm soon]. (used as the predicate nominative)
Do you know [who the composer was]? (used as the direct object)
Hand these brochures to [whoever wants them]. (used as the object of a preposition)

Notice that, just like adjective clauses, noun clauses also begin with relatives. Also, just as in an adjective clause, a relative in a noun clause will almost always serve some specific grammatical function within the noun clause. In addition to the relatives commonly used in adjective clauses (*who, whom, whose, which, that, when, where*), add a few more: *what, whatever, whoever, whomever, whichever*.

I did not understand [*what* he said].
The verb in the noun clause is *said*.
The subject of *said* is *he*.
The relative *what* is the direct object.
The entire dependent clause is used as a noun, specifically as the direct object of *did understand*, the verb in the independent clause.

Note that, unlike relatives in adjective clauses, the relative in a noun clause does not have a specific antecedent.

Just as with adjective clauses, sometimes the relative in a noun clause may be omitted. Again you may wish to put in an appropriate relative to help you analyze the clause correctly.

I forgot [our paper was due tomorrow]. (The relative *that* has been omitted from the beginning of the noun clause.)

The use of relatives to begin adjective and noun clauses is so much a traditional part of English usage that English speakers use relatives even when they really serve no specific grammatical function in the noun clause. In such cases, the relative's only function is to signal the beginning of the dependent clause.

> My advisor told me [*that* Old Testament Survey is a required course].
>> The verb in the noun clause is *is*.
>> The subject of *is* is *Old Testament Survey*.
>> *Course* is the predicate nominative.
>> The relative *that* really has no grammatical function in the clause, but it does signal the beginning of the noun clause.

Students sometimes confuse two types of clauses that look quite similar but are, in fact, quite different. Examine these two sentences:

> Scholars have not determined [to *whom* the epistle was addressed].
> The woman [to *whom* the epistle was addressed] clearly was wealthy and influential.

The very same group of words serves as two different parts of speech: in the first sentence as a noun used as the direct object of the verb *have determined*, in the second sentence as an adjective modifying the noun *woman*.

Distinguishing between adjective and noun clauses may become particularly challenging in certain circumstances. This may even lead to questions about pronoun usage. Consider this sentence:

> We will give the vegetables to (whoever, whomever) wants them.

Should the pronoun be *whoever* or *whomever*? *Whoever* is a pronoun in the nominative case and should be used for a subject or a predicate nominative. *Whomever* is a pronoun in the objective case and should be used for any type of object. Which is correct in this sentence?

> The two verbs in the sentence are *will give* and *wants*.
> The subject of *will give* is *We*.
> The subject of *wants* is *whoever/whomever*; hence, the correct pronoun is *whoever*.
> The dependent clause is *whoever wants them*.
> The dependent clause is therefore a noun clause used as the object of the preposition *to*.
> Note that the preposition *to* would not be included in the dependent clause. The preposition cannot be part of its own object.

Now consider this sentence:

> Police have not yet identified for (who, whom) the package was intended.

Should the pronoun be *who* or *whom*? *Who* is a pronoun in the nominative case (used for subjects and predicate nominatives), and *whom* is a pronoun in the objective case (used for objects). Which is correct in this sentence?

> The two verbs in the sentence are *have identified* and *was intended*.
> The subject of *have identified* is *Police*.
> The subject of *was intended* is *package*.
> The pronoun *who/whom* is the object of the preposition *for*; hence, the correct pronoun is *whom*.
> The dependent clause is *for whom the package was intended*, and it is a noun clause used as the direct object of the verb *have identified*.

As noted in Chapter 1, some modern educators have asserted that the study of traditional grammar is totally unrelated to the study of composition. Obviously even this little demonstration shows the utter absurdity of that assertion. No one who does not understand English syntax can possibly write clearly and effectively, much less correctly.

Adverb Clause

A dependent clause can also be used as an adverb. Like any adverb, an adverb clause will modify a verb, an adjective, or an adverb.

> The soldiers returned home [after the war ended]. (modifies the verb *returned*)
> Are you sure [that these mattresses are on sale]? (modifies the adjective *sure*)
> David ran faster [than the other runners]. (modifies the adverb *faster*)

Whereas adjective and noun clauses begin with relatives, adverb clauses start with subordinating conjunctions. Become familiar with this list of common subordinating conjunctions.

after	before	than	whenever
although	if	that	where
as	in order that	though	wherever
as if	lest	unless	whether
as ... as (e.g., *as much as*)	since	until	while
because	so that	when	

Unlike relatives, subordinating conjunctions serve only a very limited grammatical function within the dependent clause. They connect the adverb clause to the independent clause, and they indicate—to some extent—the relationship of the dependent clause to the verb, adjective, or adverb being modified.

Adverb clauses that modify the verb are frequently located at the beginning of the sentence and are usually set off by a comma.

> Because I could not stop for Death, he kindly stopped for me.
> –Emily Dickinson

Sometimes part of an adverb clause is omitted, especially after the subordinating conjunctions *than* and *as*. This is called an elliptical clause. You may wish to put back in the omitted words to help you in analyzing the clause.

> The cheetah can run faster [than a racehorse]. (The verb *can run* has been omitted.)
> Are you as tall [as your sister]? (The verb *is* has been omitted.)

Types of Sentences

Sentences can be classified according to function. Declarative sentences make statements. Interrogative sentences ask questions. Imperative sentences make commands or requests. Exclamatory sentences make exclamations.

However, for the purposes of sentence analysis, the best way to classify sentences is by their structure. Sentences can be classified as simple, compound, complex, or compound-complex. They are classified on the basis of how many independent and dependent clauses they have.

A simple sentence has one independent clause and no dependent clauses. Do not let the term *simple* mislead you. A simple sentence may have numerous prepositional phrases, verbals, or appositives. It may have a compound subject or compound verb.

> The whip-poor-will flew farther into the forest and took up his lament again, sweet with distance. –Marjorie Kinnan Rawlings

A compound sentence has two or more independent clauses and no dependent clauses. The two independent clauses may be joined either by a comma and a coordinating conjunction (*and, but, or, nor, for, yet, so*) or by a semicolon.

> He spake**, and** it was done. –Psalm 33:9
> Beware of expenses**;** a small leak will sink a great ship. –Benjamin Franklin

A complex sentence has only one independent clause and one or more dependent clauses.

> There was a man in the land of Uz, [whose name was Job]. –Job 1:1

A compound-complex sentence is both compound and complex. A compound sentence, it contains two or more independent clauses. A complex sentence, it contains one or more dependent clauses.

> Eternity to the godly is a day [that has no sunset]**;** eternity to the wicked is a night [that has no sunrise]. –Thomas Watson

Chapter 4
The Verb and Its Usage

Principal Parts

Verbs have four principal parts, called the present (or present infinitive), the present participle, the past, and the past participle. Virtually all forms of the verb are formed from these four principal (or primary) parts.

Even in quite ancient times, when English was the language only of the Angles and Saxons (who invaded Britain in the year AD 449), there were two types of English verbs. Those two types of verbs have come to be called regular and irregular verbs. Regular verbs form their past and past participle forms by adding *ed* (or sometimes merely *d* or *t*) to the present (or present infinitive) form.

present	**present participle**	**past**	**past participle**
appear	appearing	appeared	appeared
love	loving	loved	loved
burn	burning	burned	burnt
mean	meaning	meant	meant

Irregular verbs form their past and past participle forms in some other way, often by changing a vowel. (Actually, it is somewhat inaccurate to call the second type "irregular" with the implication that they are somehow defective. Many of the so-called "irregular" verbs are ancient Anglo-Saxon verbs and have always formed their principal parts by changing the spelling rather than by adding *d* or *ed*.)

present	**present participle**	**past**	**past participle**
drink	drinking	drank	drunk
buy	buying	bought	bought
freeze	freezing	froze	frozen
set	setting	set	set

Even though these are "irregular," there is some pattern to these changes. Notice that verbs which end in a silent *e* generally drop the *e* before adding *ing*.

change	changing
love	loving

Verbs which end in *y* preceded by a consonant change the *y* to *i* before adding *ed*.

supply	supplied
deny	denied

Verbs which end in a single consonant preceded by an accented short vowel double the final consonant before adding *ing* or *ed*.

refer	referring	referred	(last syllable is accented)
marvel	marveling	marveled	(last syllable is not accented)

The present participle of both regular and irregular verbs is formed merely by adding *ing* to the present (or present infinitive) form.

Most errors in verb usage are made because speakers or writers do not know the four principal parts of irregular verbs. Become very familiar with this list of common irregular verbs and their four principal parts.

present	**present participle**	**past**	**past participle**
beat	beating	beat	beaten
begin	beginning	began	begun
bite	biting	bit	bitten
blow	blowing	blew	blown
break	breaking	broke	broken
bring	bringing	brought	brought
build	building	built	built
burst	bursting	burst	burst
buy	buying	bought	bought
choose	choosing	chose	chosen
come	coming	came	come
do	doing	did	done
draw	drawing	drew	drawn

drink	drinking	drank	drunk
eat	eating	ate	eaten
fall	falling	fell	fallen
fly	flying	flew	flown
freeze	freezing	froze	frozen
get	getting	got	got/gotten
give	giving	gave	given
go	going	went	gone
grow	growing	grew	grown
hold	holding	held	held
know	knowing	knew	known
lay	laying	laid	laid
lead	leading	led	led
leave	leaving	left	left
lie	lying	lay	lain
lose	losing	lost	lost
pay	paying	paid	paid
ride	riding	rode	ridden
ring	ringing	rang	rung
rise	rising	rose	risen
run	running	ran	run
say	saying	said	said
see	seeing	saw	seen
set	setting	set	set
shake	shaking	shook	shaken
show	showing	showed	shown
shrink	shrinking	shrank	shrunk
sing	singing	sang	sung
sink	sinking	sank	sunk
sit	sitting	sat	sat
speak	speaking	spoke	spoken
spring	springing	sprang	sprung
steal	stealing	stole	stolen
swear	swearing	swore	sworn
swim	swimming	swam	swum
take	taking	took	taken
tear	tearing	tore	torn
think	thinking	thought	thought
throw	throwing	threw	thrown
wear	wearing	wore	worn
weep	weeping	wept	wept
win	winning	won	won
write	writing	wrote	written

By studying these common irregular verbs you will learn to avoid such incorrect forms as *brung, busted, drownd, drownded, drug, growed, lead* (for *led*), *snuck, stoled,* and *throwed*.

> The dog *dragged* a board around the yard. (not *drug*)
> Burglars *sneaked* into the darkened home. (not *snuck*)
> Who *led* the English troops at Agincourt? (not *lead*)

Be careful not to switch the past and past participle forms. The past form is not used with helping verbs.

> Bobby *did* a good job on his research paper. (not *done*)
> I *saw* him as he entered the house. (not *seen*)
> *Had* he *gone* already? (not *had went*)

Troublesome Verbs

There are, however, three pairs of verbs which, because of certain irregular forms and similar spelling, are especially troublesome. They are *sit* and *set*, *rise* and *raise*, and *lie* and *lay*.

Sit/Set

The verb *sit* means "to be seated," as in a chair. Its principal parts are *sit, sitting, sat, (have) sat*. Notice that *sit* is an intransitive verb and therefore does not take a direct object, nor can it be made passive.

> Which pew *do* you usually *sit* on?
> The weary boys *were sitting* on the front porch.
> The poor man *sat* down and put his head in his hands.
> This clock *has sat* in this same spot for over a hundred years.

The verb *set* means "to put or place." Its principal parts are *set, setting, set, (have) set*. Notice that *set* is a transitive verb and therefore does take a direct object and can be made passive.

> My father usually *sets* his wallet on his chest-of-drawers.
> We *are setting* out the tomato plants today.
> Jennifer *set* the basket of laundry in the kitchen.
> *Have* you *set* the table yet?

Rise/Raise

The verb *rise* means "to go up" or "to get up." Its principal parts are *rise, rising, rose, (have) risen*. Notice that *rise* is an intransitive verb and therefore does not take a direct object, nor can it be made passive.

> Jesus *rises* from supper and begins to wash the disciples' feet.
> The balloon *was rising* higher into the sky.
> The river *rose* dangerously high overnight.
> The sun *had risen* already.

The verb *raise* means "to lift something" or "to move something upward." Its principal parts are *raise, raising, raised, (have) raised*. Notice that it is a transitive verb and therefore does take a direct object and can be made passive.

> *Raise* your hand if you have a question.
> The honor guard *was raising* the flag.
> The workmen *raised* the frame of the barn in a few hours.
> *Has* anyone *raised* any objection?

Lie/Lay

The verbs *lie* and *lay* are particularly troublesome. Their forms are very similar but not the same, and they are easily confused. The verb *lie* means "to recline" or "to rest." Its principal parts are *lie, lying, lay, (have) lain*. Notice that it is an intransitive verb and therefore does not take a direct object, nor can it be made passive.

> *Lie* down and take a nap.
> The papers *were lying* right where I had left them.
> Frank *lay* under the tree and rested.
> The injured soldier *had lain* on the battlefield for hours.

The verb *lay* means "to put or place." Its principal parts are *lay, laying, laid, (have) laid*. Notice that it is a transitive verb and therefore does take a direct object and can be made passive.

> *Lay* down your weapons!
> We *will be laying* the foundation for the new house tomorrow.
> The child *laid* his head in his mother's lap.
> The hands of the high priest *were laid* on the head of the goat.

Tense

The English word *tense* comes, by way of French, from the Latin word *tempus*, meaning "time." Every verb in English has six tenses or "times" at which it can be expressed. The six verb tenses in English are present, past, future (sometimes called the "simple tenses") and past, past perfect (or pluperfect), and future perfect. For an example, look at this listing of all the tense forms of the verb *love*. A listing of all the tense forms of a verb is called the conjugation of the verb.

Conjugation of the Verb *To Love*[1]

Principal Parts

present	**present participle**	**past**	**past participle**
love	loving	loved	loved

Present Tense

	singular	**plural**
first person	I love	we love
second person	you love	you love
third person	he/she/it loves	they love

Present Progressive: I am loving, you are loving, etc.
Present Emphatic: I do love, you do love, etc.

Past Tense

	singular	**plural**
first person	I loved	we loved
second person	you loved	you loved
third person	he/she/it loved	they loved

Past Progressive: I was loving, you were loving, etc.
Past Emphatic: I did love, you did love, etc.

Future Tense

	singular	**plural**
first person	I shall/will love	we shall/will love
second person	you will/shall love	you will/shall love
third person	he/she/it will/shall love	they will/shall love

Future Progressive: I shall be loving, you will be loving, etc.

---

[1] Technically, this is the conjugation of the verb *to love* only in the indicative mood, active voice. There are two other moods (imperative and subjunctive) and another voice (passive). A discussion of both mood and voice will follow later in this chapter.

Present Perfect Tense

	singular	plural
first person	I have loved	we have loved
second person	you have loved	you have loved
third person	he/she/it has loved	they have loved

Present Perfect Progressive: I have been loving, you have been loving, etc.

Past Perfect Tense

	singular	plural
first person	I had loved	we had loved
second person	you had loved	you had loved
third person	he/she/it had loved	they had loved

Past Perfect Progressive: I had been loving, you had been loving, etc.

Future Perfect Tense

	singular	plural
first person	I shall/will have loved	we shall/will have loved
second person	you will/shall have loved	you will/shall have loved
third person	he/she/it will/shall have loved	they will/shall have loved

Future Perfect Progressive: I shall have been loving, you will have been loving, etc.

You will immediately notice several important things about verb tenses:

Each tense comes in three "persons": first person, second person, and third person. First person is the person speaking (*I* or *we*). Second person is the person being spoken to (*you* singular or *you* plural). Third person is the person being spoken about (*he, she, it*, or *they*).

These persons come in singular and plural. The singular persons are *I, you, he, she*, and *it*. The plural persons are *we, you*, and *they*.

Each tense, in addition to its regular forms, also has a "progressive" form. This form is used to indicate a continuing action or an action in progress. It is expressed by using a form of the verb *to be* (*am, is, are, was, were, be, being, been*) and the present participle.

> We *are finishing* the dishes now.
> They *were* still *running* toward class when the bell rang.

The progressive form is of comparatively recent origin: though occurring in Middle English, it did not reach wide usage until the sixteenth century in the early Modern period. For a while it was common to indicate continuous action by using the preposition *on* followed by the present participle (e.g., *he burst out on laughing*). Gradually, this developed into *he burst out a-laughing* and then to *he burst out laughing*. Similarly, *he was on laughing* developed into *he was a-laughing* and then *he was laughing*. The development of the progressive in the passive voice occurred even later, as late as the eighteenth century. (So far, the language has developed the progressive forms in the passive voice in the present and past tenses only.)[2]

Additionally, the present and past tenses (but no others) have another form, called the emphatic. This form is used generally to indicate special emphasis. It is expressed by using a form of the verb *to do* (*do, does, did*) and the first principal part. It is also frequently used for asking questions.

> Yes, I *did* work in New Orleans for several years.
> *Do* you *take* any chemistry classes?

In order to use the six different tenses correctly, it is important to understand how each is constructed and what each indicates.

Present tense is used to indicate an action (or to make a statement about something) that is occurring now, at the present time.

> We *live* on Old Charlotte Pike.
> My brother *is* a pastor in Alabama.

In addition to its main use, present tense also has several other uses.

Present tense can be used to indicate a customary or habitual action or state.

> Our family always *prays* before meals.

Present tense can be used to indicate a general truth, something that is true at all times.

> Copernicus asserted that the earth *orbits* the sun.

[2] Albert C. Baugh and Thomas Cable, *A History of the English Language*, fifth edition (Upper Saddle River, NJ: Prentice Hall, 2002), 292-293.

Present tense can be used to discuss events of the past as if they were present. This is done to make the discussion particularly lively and vivid. It is sometimes called historical present.

> Trusting in God's direction, Abraham *leaves* the city of Ur and *sets* out toward the west.

Present tense is frequently used in a discussion of literature. This is sometimes called literary present.

> Shakespeare *describes* fools who "put an enemy in their mouths to steal away their brains."
> In this poem Herbert *reminds* us that nature is a window for observing the hand of God.
> By the end of the *Iliad*, Achilles *is* a changed man, still a mighty warrior, but humbler and wiser.

Present tense is sometimes used in common speech to express the future.

> His plane *leaves* Monday morning at 8:00.
> The fall term *begins* on August 28.

The past tense is used to indicate an action (or to make a statement about something) that occurred at a definite time in the past.

> The Japanese *attacked* Pearl Harbor on Sunday, December 7, 1941.
> Charles I *ruled* from his father's death in 1625 until his execution by Parliament in 1649.

The future tense is used to indicate an action (or to make a statement about something) that will occur in the future. The helping verbs *shall* and *will* are now used interchangeably to indicate the future tense.

> On Saturday, the Student Council *will sponsor* a work day in the college garden.

It used to be the custom among educated users of English to use *shall* normally in the first person (both singular and plural) and to use *will* in the second and third persons. To indicate great emphasis, the helping verbs were reversed, with *will* used in the first person and *shall* used in the second and third persons. Thus, an earlier speaker of English might have said, "I *shall leave* tomorrow morning." If someone had forbidden him from going, he might have responded, "No, I *will leave* tomorrow morning!" You may still find this usage in earlier works of literature; however, this helpful distinction between *shall* and *will* is unfortunately rarely made today.

Future tense may also be indicated by using a present tense form of the verb *to be* with the word *going* plus an infinitive.

> Ellen *is going* to study the piano.
> I *am going* to be sick!

The present perfect tense is used to indicate an action (or to make a statement about something) that began in the past but has been completed in the present. It is formed by the helping verbs *have* or *has* and the past participle.

> Mr. Forlines *has taught* at the college for over forty years.
> *Have* you *completed* your research paper yet?

The past perfect tense (sometimes called the pluperfect tense) is used to indicate an action (or to make a statement about something) that was completed in the past before some other past action or event. It is formed by the helping verb *had* and the past participle.

> After I *had finished* my research, I constructed a final outline for my paper.

The future perfect tense is used to indicate an action (or to make a statement about something) that will be completed in the future before some other future action or event. It is formed by the helping verbs *shall have* or *will have* and the past participle.

> By the end of this term, I *shall have taught* twenty-six years.
> When he arrives tomorrow, we *will* already *have completed* registration.

Tense Sequence

Usually it is not difficult to know which verb tense to use. However, if the sentence contains a verbal phrase or a dependent clause, the exact time relationship between the main verb and the subordinate verb may be unclear. Examine the verb tenses carefully to make sure that they express a logical time relationship.

Use past perfect tense to indicate an action or event that occurred before some other action or event in the past.

After I *had completed* my first draft, I edited it for grammar and mechanical errors. (The completing of the first draft occurred in the past but before the editing.)
As the governor *entered* the room, the reporters stood up. (The governor's entering and the reporters' standing up occurred at the same time.)

Even if an action or event is merely hypothetical and contrary-to-fact, even if it only theoretically occurred further back in the past than another past action or event, still use past perfect tense. Do not use *would have*.

If you *had listened* to me, this would not have happened. (The listening—though theoretical—would have occurred before the happening.)

When using verbals, be careful to maintain the logical time relationship with the main verb in the sentence.

A present infinitive and a present participle indicate that the action occurs at the same time as the main verb or at a later time.

The spy claimed *to know* the enemies' plans. (The claiming and the knowing occur at the same time.)
Ben hoped *to see* us at the family reunion. (Ben did not hope to have already seen us; rather he hoped to see us in the future.)
Looking into the pine tree, I saw the turkey perched on a limb. (The looking occurs at the same time as the seeing.)

A past (or perfect) infinitive (such as *to have loved, to have gone*, etc.) and a past (or perfect) participle (such as *having loved, having gone*, etc.) indicate that the action occurred at a time before the time of the main verb.

The pioneers were happy *to have crossed* the mountains. (Crossing the mountains occurred before the pioneers became happy.)
Having read Johnson's new book on evolution, I understand the flaws of Darwinism better now. (The reading occurred before the understanding.)

Voice

In addition to having tense, verbs also have voice. The six tenses indicate the six times which a verb can express in English. The two voices indicate the two relationships a verb can have with its subject. A verb can have active voice or passive voice. All verbs can be divided into two main types: action verbs and linking verbs. Action verbs involve some type of physical, mental, or emotional action (*eat, plow, think, meditate, read, fear*). Linking verbs are used to link the subject to the rest of the predicate (perhaps a complement such as a predicate nominative or a predicate adjective). All action verbs are said to be transitive or intransitive, depending on whether anything is receiving the action of the verb. (Linking verbs, of course, cannot be said to be transitive or intransitive since they do not show action at all.) Action verbs are described as intransitive when neither a direct object nor the subject receives the action of the verb. The term *intransitive* comes from the Latin verb *transire*, meaning "to move across" and the Latin prefix *in*, meaning "not." In a sentence with an intransitive verb, though there is action shown, there is no transfer of action; nothing receives the action.

> Upon hearing the terrible news, my mother wept. (The verb *wept* is certainly an action, but nothing receives the action. The subject does the action, but there is no receiver of the action. *Wept* is an intransitive action verb.)

Action verbs are described as transitive when either a direct object or the subject receives the action of the verb.

> The hunter *shot* the quail. (*Quail* is the direct object of the transitive action verb *shot*.)
> The quail *were shot* by the hunter. (*Quail* is the subject of the transitive action verb *were shot*.)

When a direct object receives the action of the transitive action verb, the verb is said to have active voice. When the subject receives the action of the transitive action verb, the verb is said to have passive voice.

> Bees *make* honey from the nectar of flowers. (Active voice—the direct object *honey* receives the action of the transitive action verb *make*)
> Honey *is made* by bees from the nectar of flowers. (Passive voice—the subject *honey* receives the action of the transitive action verb *is made*)

A passive voice verb is constructed by using the past participle (which ends in *ed, en, t*, etc.) with a form of the verb *to be* as a helping verb (*am, is, are, was, were, be, being, been*). Of course, other helping verbs will be used with these to construct the various verb tenses.

> The Latin language *is studied* by the students. (present tense, passive voice)
> The Latin language *was studied* by the students. (past tense, passive voice)
> The Latin language *will be studied* by the students. (future tense, passive voice)
> The Latin language *has been studied* by the students. (present perfect tense, passive voice)

The Latin language *had been studied* by the students. (past perfect tense, passive voice)
The Latin language *will have been studied* by the students. (future perfect tense, passive voice)

Examine this conjugation of the verb *to love* in the passive voice.

Conjugation of the Verb *To Love*[3]
Passive Voice

Present Tense

	singular	**plural**
first person	I am loved	we are loved
second person	you are loved	you are loved
third person	he/she/it is loved	they are loved

Present Progressive: I am being loved, you are being loved, etc.

Past Tense

	singular	**plural**
first person	I was loved	we were loved
second person	you were loved	you were loved
third person	he/she/it was loved	they were loved

Past Progressive: I was being loved, you were being loved, etc.

Future Tense

	singular	**plural**
first person	I shall/will be loved	we shall/will be loved
second person	you will/shall be loved	you will/shall be loved
third person	he/she/it will/shall be loved	they will/shall be loved

Present Perfect Tense

	singular	**plural**
first person	I have been loved	we have been loved
second person	you have been loved	you have been loved
third person	he/she/it has been loved	they have been loved

Past Perfect Tense

	singular	**plural**
first person	I had been loved	we had been loved
second person	you had been loved	you had been loved
third person	he/she/it had been loved	they had been loved

[3] Technically, this is the conjugation of the verb *to love* only in the indicative mood, passive voice. A discussion of other moods will follow later in the chapter.

Future Perfect Tense

	singular	plural
first person	I shall/will have been loved	we shall/will have been loved
second person	you will/shall have been loved	you will/shall have been loved
third person	he/she/it will/shall have been loved	they will/shall have been loved

A sentence can be stated in either active or passive voice. Consider these two sentences:

The mechanic *repaired* the truck. (active voice)
The truck *was repaired* by the mechanic. (passive voice)

Basically, these two sentences say the very same thing. However, the passive voice is well named. It indicates a certain passivity which should be used only sparingly. The overuse of passive voice may make your writing seem weak or awkward. Do not, however, be afraid to use the passive voice when it is appropriate.

Use the passive voice if you do not know the doer of the action.

Something *was spilled* on the living room carpet.
The baby kangaroo *is called* a joey.

Use the passive voice if the receiver of the action is more important than the doer of the action.

The Dead Sea Scrolls *were discovered* in 1947 quite by accident by a Bedouin boy searching for lost sheep. (In a paper on Biblical manuscripts, the Dead Sea Scrolls themselves would be of more importance than the name of the boy who accidentally discovered them.)

Use the passive voice to omit the doer of the action intentionally.

No doubt the matter *was* not *handled* as well as it might have been.
Mistakes *were made*.

Mood

In addition to tense and voice, a verb also has mood. The three moods of a verb are the indicative mood, the imperative mood, and the subjunctive mood. These are appropriately called "moods," for they indicate the different manners in which a statement may be made.

Indicative mood makes a statement of fact or asks a question. This is the "normal" mood used most of the time.

> Modern critical methods frequently *ignore* the plain meaning of a literary text.
> *Have* you ever *visited* the Grand Canyon?

See the earlier presentation of the conjugation of a verb in the indicative mood.

Imperative mood gives a command or makes a request.

> *Sit* down.
> Using your microscopes, please *examine* the cell's nucleus.

In English, there is only one form of the imperative; it is the same as the first principal part.

Subjunctive mood implies that an action or condition is not a reality. In earlier forms of English, the subjunctive mood was much more widely used than it is today.[4] The language has simplified so much that today the subjunctive mood is generally exactly like the indicative mood in form—with only two primary exceptions.

(1) In the present and past tenses, the verb *to be* is conjugated as follows in the subjunctive mood:

	Present Tense	
	singular	**plural**
first person	I be	we be
second person	you be	you be
third person	he/she/it be	they be

[4] Some of these earlier subjunctive uses still survive, especially in high historical or literary settings. Consider such expressions as the following: *glory be, good-bye (God be with ye), God bless you, God save the king, Heaven preserve us, the Lord have mercy, long live the king, far be it from me, suffice it to say, albeit (although + be + it)*. Cf. Otto Jespersen, *Essentials of English Grammar* (University, AL: University of Alabama, 1966), 293-294.

	Past Tense	
	singular	**plural**
first person	I were	we were
second person	you were	you were
third person	he/she/it were	they were

In all the other four tenses, the verb *to be* is conjugated in the subjunctive mood just as it is conjugated in the indicative mood.

(2) All other verbs in the language make only one change between their indicative forms and their subjunctive forms. In the present tense, third person, singular, they drop the *s* or *es* from the indicative mood form to form the subjunctive. Hence, *he loves* becomes *he love*, and *she does* becomes *she do*.

Basically, there are now only four times to use these specifically subjunctive mood forms.

Use subjunctive mood in a dependent clause expressing a condition to indicate that the condition is actually unreal or contrary-to-fact.

> If I *were* president, I would appoint judges who interpreted the Constitution strictly. (But, alas, I am not the president.)
> If Marcus *were* more serious about his studies, I am sure he would improve his grades. (But, unfortunately, Marcus is not serious about his studies.)

Use subjunctive mood in a dependent clause after the subordinating conjunctions *as if* or *as though*.

> Ashley looked as if she *were* about to say something.

Use subjunctive mood in a dependent clause to express a wish, a request, or a requirement.

> I wish that it *were* time for dinner.
> Dan's father requested that he *mow* the yard.
> My parents always insisted that I *be* home before midnight.

Use subjunctive mood in a dependent clause to state a parliamentary motion or a legal judgment.

> I move that this issue *be tabled* until a later date.
> The judge's decision was that the property *be sold* and that the proceeds *be divided* among the heirs.

Auxiliary Verbs

Certain English verb phrases consist of a main verb and an auxiliary (or helping) verb. The most common auxiliary verbs are *am, is, are, was, were, be, being, been, have, having, has, had, do, does, did, must, can, could, may, might, shall, will, should, would.* Care should be taken in the use of auxiliary verbs since they indicate fine shades of meaning.

Am, Is, Are, Was, Were, Be, Being, Been

Use the forms of the verb *to be* to form the progressive form in all tenses and to form the passive voice.

> When I found them, they *were strolling* in the garden. (progressive)
> Achsah *was given* land by her father Caleb. (passive)

Have, Having, Has, Had

Use the forms of the verb *to have* to form the present perfect tense (*I have loved, she has loved*), the past perfect tense (*I had loved*), the future perfect tense (*I shall have loved, you will have loved*), the past tense of the participle (*having loved, having been loved*), and the past tense of the infinitive (*to have loved, to have been loved*).

Do, Does, Did

Use the forms of the verb *to do* to form the emphatic form in the present and past tenses and to ask certain questions.

> Yes, I *do live* in Tennessee now.
> *Did* you *find* the address?

Must

Use *must* to indicate necessity.

> Illegal immigrants *must* not *be permitted* to remain in the country.

Can, Could

Use *can* (present tense) and *could* (past tense) to indicate ability.

> *Can* you *speak* Spanish fluently? (present tense)
> *Could* he *find* the book he was looking for? (past tense)

Use *could* to indicate ability in conditions. (Actually, this is a subjunctive mood usage.)

> If I *could go*, I would.

May, Might

Use *may* (present tense) and *might* (past tense) to indicate permission, liberty, or likelihood.

> *May* I *have* another glass of tea?
> You *may* not *go* out of town overnight without informing the dean.
> Nicholson's hypothesis *may be* correct.
> He *might have been* out of town at the time.

Use *may* (present tense) and *might* (past tense) to express certain wishes. (These too are subjunctive uses.)

> *May* the best man *win*! (present tense)
> Our Lord prayed that the Father's will *might be done*.
> I wish that I *may* never *hear* of it again! (present tense)
> He wished that he *might* never *hear* of it again. (past tense)

Shall, Will

Use *shall* and *will* to form the future and future perfect tenses. These auxiliary verb forms are now used practically interchangeably.

> I *will be* glad and *rejoice* in Thee; I *will sing* praise to Thy name, O Thou most High. –Psalm 9:2

Should, Would

Use *should* to express duty or necessity, much like *ought*.

> You should finish your homework first.

Use *should* to express likelihood, especially of a desirable event or occurrence.

> He *should be* available this afternoon.
> Interest rates *should* moderate somewhat at the beginning of next year.

Use *should* in a relative clause beginning with *that* to indicate an expression of opinion. (This is a subjunctive usage.)

> I am surprised that you *should feel* that way.

Use *should* to express a future condition. (This too is a subjunctive usage.)

If the price of gasoline *should continue* to rise, it will no doubt affect our driving habits.

Use *would* to express a preference, especially with *rather* or *sooner* (also a subjunctive usage).

His flock *would rather* let him starve than increase the living by one penny. –Emily Bronte
I *would sooner* die than ask him for any financial help.
As ye *would* that men should do to you, do ye also to them likewise. –Luke 6:31

Use *would* to express an intention.

We decided that we *would visit* our family in Virginia.

Use *would* to express an inclination (a subjunctive usage).

I *would like* to recommend an alternative.
Would you *care* for more peach cobbler?
He *would* not *listen* to my advice.

Use *would* to express habitual or customary action in the past.

When I was a boy, we *would* often *go* to the swimming hole on Saturday afternoon.

Use *would* as the result of a condition (a subjunctive usage).

If the Kurds should declare independence, how *would* Turkey *respond*?
If my father were alive, he *would* certainly not *approve* of this.

Use *would* in a noun clause to express a wish or desire (a subjunctive usage).

Churchill hoped that the United States *would enter* the war as well.

Use *would* to indicate the future in indirect discourse.

General Macarthur told the Filipinos that he *would return*.
She said that she *would be* glad to help me.
She asked whether you *would like* to go.

Subject-Verb Agreement

One area of some concern is subject-verb agreement. Verbs must agree with their subjects in number. Number simply means whether the word is singular or plural. Singular subjects must take singular verbs, and plural subjects must take plural verbs. By this point in your education you no doubt have very little trouble distinguishing singular and plural nouns and singular and plural verbs. It may be helpful to remember that nouns that end in *s* are plural and verbs that end in *s* are singular.

> The *girl sings* in the choir. (singular)
> The *girls sing* in the choir. (plural)

The number of the subject is not usually affected by a phrase which may come between the subject and verb.

> This *collection* of short stories *is* by Flannery O'Connor. (singular)
> The *stories* included in this book *reveal* O'Connor's interest in Christian theology. (plural)
> Our *school*, along with several others in the city, *sponsors* a yearly book fair. (singular)

Remember that verbs agree with their subjects, not with their predicate nominatives.

> His favorite *fruit is* peaches. (The verb agrees with the singular subject *fruit*, not the plural predicate nominative *peaches*.)

There and *here* are not nouns and cannot be used as subjects. If a sentence starts with one of these words, look carefully to locate the subject.

> Here *are* the *files* you wanted. (The plural noun *files* is the subject.)
> There *is* the *book* I was looking for. (The singular noun *book* is the subject.)

Titles of literary and other artistic works, as well as names of organizations and places (cities, countries, etc.) are singular, even if they contain plural words.

> Plutarch's *Lives of the Noble Greeks and Romans was* the source of several of Shakespeare's plays.
> *Chariots of Fire shows* Eric Liddell's famous race in the 1924 Olympics.
> "June Apples," an old Appalachian tune, *was* played on the fiddle.
> The Netherlands *has* a constitutional monarch.

Sioux Falls *is located* in South Dakota.

Names of diseases, though plural in form, are actually singular.

Measles *was* once a common cause of death.
Mumps produces swelling of the parotid glands, located below the ears.

Collective nouns can be singular or plural, depending on their use in the sentence. Usually there will be enough context in the sentence to let you know whether it is being thought of as a single unit (which would be singular) or as numerous individuals (which would be plural).

The faculty *meets* the first Monday afternoon of each month. (singular—the faculty meets as one group)
In the meeting, the faculty *were* expressing their opinions on the new grading scale. (plural—*their opinions* indicates plurality)

Words expressing amounts (such as fractions, measurements, money, and time) may be singular or plural, depending on their use in the sentence. If the amount refers to one thing (such as a price or a distance) it will be singular. If the amount refers to numerous individual items, it will be plural. Fractions are frequently followed by prepositional phrases which indicate whether they should be understood as singular or plural. If you can count the items included in a fraction, it is plural; if not, it is singular.

Three hundred dollars *is* too much to spend for that suit.
Three fourths of the homes in the small town *were* destroyed by the tornado.
Three fourths of the flour *was* contaminated.

Generally, words that end in *–ics* are considered singular if they refer to a science or course of study which one might take in school, but are otherwise plural.

Economics *has* been described as "the dismal science." (singular)
Civics *is* designed to teach the basics of American government. (singular)
Does ethics include a study of natural rights? (singular)
Their so-called ethics *do* not prevent them from taking innocent life. (plural)
The boys' gymnastics *were* amazing to watch. (plural)

Since 1 and 1 make 2, two (or more) singular subjects joined by *and* are plural.

> Jared and Emily *are* our class's representatives on the Student Council.

However, if the two subjects joined by *and* refer to only one person or thing, they are singular.

> Our society's secretary and treasurer *is* Kathleen.
> Chicken and dumplings *is* the main dish in the cafeteria today.

Two (or more) singular subjects joined by *or* or *nor* are singular.

> Either the librarian or her assistant *is* always present to help students in their research.

If one of two singular subjects joined by *or* or *nor* is singular and the other plural, make the verb agree with the subject nearer to it.

> Either the librarian or her student assistants *are* always present to help students in their research. (plural)
> Either the student assistants or the librarian herself *is* always present to help students in their research. (singular)

This chart on subject-verb agreement may be helpful:

subject	**verb**
S	S
P	P
S and S	P
P and P	P
S and P	P
P and S	P
S or S	S
P or P	P
S or P	P
P or S	S

If the subject of the verb is an indefinite pronoun, care should be taken. Some indefinite pronouns are singular, some are plural, and some can be singular or plural, depending on their use in the sentence.

These indefinite pronouns are always singular: *each, either, neither, one*, and all that end in *–one* or *–body* (*anyone, everyone, no one, someone, anybody, everybody, nobody, somebody*).

> Someone *has* parked in the tow-away zone next to the mailbox.
> Each of the boys *was* reprimanded for the vandalism.
> Everyone *is* invited to the auction.

These indefinite pronouns are always plural: *both, few, several, many*.

> Both of the rivers *have* risen considerably as a result of the recent rains.
> Several of their children *have* red hair.

Some indefinite pronouns are sometimes singular and sometimes plural, depending on their use in the sentence. They are *some, any, none, all, most*. They frequently are followed by prepositional phrases which indicate whether they should be understood as singular or plural. If you can count the items in the prepositional phrase, the pronoun is plural; if not, it is singular.

> Fortunately, none of the employees *were* injured in the accident.
> Some of the produce *was* not fit to be sold.

When using contractions look carefully at the verb to see whether it is singular or plural. The fact that the verb is part of a contraction does not affect whether it is singular or plural.

> He *don't* work for us anymore. (incorrect)
> He *doesn't* work for us anymore. (correct)

> It *weren't* any of his business. (incorrect)
> It *wasn't* any of his business. (correct)

Chapter 5
Pronouns and Their Usage

Pronouns are words used in place of nouns.

One group of pronouns is called the personal pronouns.

Cases

As discussed earlier, Old English was a highly inflected language, making changes to a noun to show that it was used in different ways in a sentence (subject or predicate nominative, possessive, direct object, etc.) Happily for us, this method (which is called inflection) died out almost entirely in reference to nouns. Plural forms and possessive forms are the only vestiges of that earlier system of inflections. Generally, we use the same form of a noun regardless of how it is used in the sentence.[1]

This inflection to indicate different uses has been kept, however, for the personal pronouns. These different uses and their particular forms are called cases. Personal pronouns come in three cases: nominative, objective, and possessive. Examine this list of pronouns in their different cases.

	Nominative Case	
	singular	**plural**
first person	I	we
second person	you	you[2]
third person	he, she, it	they

---

[1] Nouns in English do have case: they can be used nominatively (as subjects and predicate nominatives), objectively (all objects and subjects of infinitives), and possessively (as possessive adjectives with an apostrophe and an *s* or just an apostrophe). Except for possession, nouns in Modern English do not indicate their change in case by changing their spelling.

[2] Different varieties or dialects of English have developed alternative forms of *you* plural. Such forms as *y'all, you all, you-uns, yous, youse*, etc. are frequently heard in different parts of America. Such forms seem to answer a very real need for a distinctly plural second person pronoun and can certainly be used in speech. However, in formal composition the pronoun *you* is used.

Objective Case

	singular	plural
first person	me	us
second person	you	you
third person	him, her, it	them

Possessive Case

	singular	plural
first person	my, mine	our, ours
second person	your, yours	your, yours
third person	his, her, hers, its	their, theirs

It may be helpful to see these personal pronouns grouped by number (singular and plural).

Singular

	nominative	objective	possessive
first person	I	me	my, mine
second person	you	you	your, yours
third person	he (masculine)	him	his
	she (feminine)	her	her, hers
	it (neuter)	it	its

Plural

	nominative	objective	possessive
first person	we	us	our, ours
second person	you	you	your, yours
third person	they	them	their, theirs

Notice a few things about the personal pronouns.

There are three cases: nominative, objective, and possessive.

Personal pronouns (like verbs) come in three varieties, depending on who is being referred to. First person is the person speaking; second person is the person being spoken to; and third person is the person being spoken about.

Notice that third person singular is broken down into separate pronouns based on gender. Pronouns that refer to males are said to be masculine. The masculine third person pronouns are *he* (nominative case), *him* (objective case), and *his* (possessive case). Pronouns that refer to females are said to be feminine. The feminine third person pronouns are *she* (nominative case), *her* (objective case), and *her, hers* (possessive case). Pronouns are called neuter (the Latin word for "neither") if they refer to things that do not have sexual gender. The neuter third person pronouns are *it* (nominative and objective cases), and *its* (possessive case). Notice, however, that the third person plural pronoun is not broken down into the various genders. *They, them, their*, and *theirs* are used to refer to all people and things, whether male, female, or neither.

Nominative case pronouns are used as subjects or predicate nominatives.

> *She* is my sister. (used as the subject)
> The performers will be Charles and *he*. (used as a predicate nominative)

Objective case pronouns are used as any type of object: direct object, indirect object, objective complement, retained object, object of a preposition, object of a verbal, etc. (You may remember too that some infinitives take subjects. The subject of an infinitive, though a "subject," is in the objective case.)

> Call *me* if you have any questions. (used as the direct object)
> The usher handed *me* a program. (used as the indirect object)
> Give the receipts to Mrs. Smith or *me*. (used as the object of a preposition)
> Seeing *me*, she called my name and waved. (used as the object of a participle)
> Dr. Deel wanted *me* to see her after class. (used as the subject of an infinitive)

Possessive case pronouns are used to show possession. You will notice that several of them come in two forms: *my* and *mine*, *your* and *yours* (singular), *her* and *hers*, *our* and *ours*, *your* and *yours* (plural), and *their* and *theirs*. The first of each of these is the one used as a possessive (actually, as an adjective) in front of a noun. The second of each may be a predicate adjective.

> *Our* house is located on Antioch Pike.
> The last brick house on the left is *ours*.
> *Ours* is the yellow house with the green roof.

> Is this *my* receipt?
> This necktie is *mine*.
> *Mine* is the red one with black stripes.

Common Problems with Personal Pronouns

Be sure to use the correct case form. First determine how the pronoun is used. If it is a subject or predicate nominative, use nominative case. If it is any type of an object (or subject of an infinitive), use objective case. If it is showing possession, use possessive case. Problems seem to increase when the pronoun is part of a compound construction.

> The secretary gave the dean and *(he, him)* a copy of the report.
>
> > The verb is *gave*.
> > The subject of *gave* is *secretary*.
> > *The secretary gave* what?
> > *Copy* is the direct object.
> > *The dean and (he, him)* comes between the action verb and the direct object and answers the question "to whom," so it is the indirect object.
> > Indirect objects take objective case.
> > The correct choice is *him*.

When a pronoun is used as an appositive, it will take the same case as the noun or pronoun it is renaming.

> Coach Phillips gave awards to the captains of the men's and women's teams, Tom and *(she, her)*.
>
> > *Tom and (she, her)* is an appositive of *captains*.
> > *Captains* is the object of the preposition *to*, so *captains* is in the objective case.
> > *Her* is in objective case and therefore the correct choice.

Use possessive case, not objective case, before a gerund.

> We certainly appreciate *(you, your)* helping us today.
>
> > *Helping* is a gerund.
> > *Helping us today* is a gerund phrase used as the direct object of *appreciate*.
> > The pronoun needs to show possession; therefore, use the possessive case pronoun *your*.

Be especially careful with the use of pronouns in elliptical clauses. You will remember that it is not uncommon for adverb clauses beginning with the subordinating conjunctions *than* or *as* to omit part of the clause. These are called elliptical clauses. If these clauses contain pronouns, analyze them very carefully to determine which case is needed.

Victor is taller than *(they, them)*.

The elliptical adverb clause is *than (they, them)*.
The complete clause would be *than (they, them) are*.
(They, Them) is the subject of the verb *are*.
Subjects take nominative case, so choose the nominative case pronoun *they*.

Who and *Whom*

Who and *whom* are not personal pronouns; rather they are interrogative pronouns (used for asking questions) or relative pronouns (used to begin adjective or noun clauses). *Who* is the nominative case form, and *whom* is the objective case form. *Whose* is the possessive case form. Sometimes it becomes difficult to know whether to use *who* or *whom*.

(Who, Whom) did you give the package to?

The verb is *did give*.
You is the subject of *did give*.
You did give what?
The package is the direct object.
(Who, Whom) is the object of the preposition *to*.
The objective case pronoun is *whom*.

The use of *who* and *whom* can be particularly troublesome when they are used as relatives in adjective or noun clauses. This is also true of *whoever* (another form of *who*) and *whomever* (another form of *whom*). However, by a methodical analysis of the sentence, you can readily determine the correct answer.

The man with *(who, whom)* John spoke is a defense attorney.

First, go through the sentence as normal, using the usual method of analysis. Find the verbs, the subjects, and the complements. Then put brackets around the dependent clause. The independent clause is *The man ... is a defense attorney*. The dependent clause is *with (who, whom) John spoke*. Within the dependent clause, the verb is *spoke* and the subject is *John*. Clearly *(who, whom)* is the object of the preposition *with*. Hence, the answer is the objective case pronoun *whom*.

Consider another example:

Give the envelope to *(whoever, whomever)* is sitting at the reception desk.

Again, using the normal method of sentence analysis, find the verbs, subjects, and complements. Put brackets around the dependent clause. The independent clause is *Give the envelope to. ...* The dependent clause is *(whoever, whomever) is sitting at the reception desk*. Is *(whoever, whomever)* the object of the preposition *to*? No, it is the subject of the verb *is sitting*, and it cannot be both. No, the dependent clause is a noun clause used as the object of the preposition *to*. Since *(whoever, whomever)* is the subject of the verb *is sitting*, it must be nominative case. Hence, the answer is the nominative case pronoun *whoever*.

Pronoun-Antecedent Agreement

An antecedent is the noun or pronoun that a pronoun refers to.

> *Uncle Walt* broke *his* arm in a fall on the ice. (The antecedent of the pronoun *his* is *Uncle Walt*.)

A pronoun must agree with its antecedent in number. Number is the quality of being singular or plural. If the antecedent is plural, the pronoun must be plural. If the antecedent is singular, the pronoun must be singular.

This may be especially troublesome if the antecedent is one of the indefinite pronouns. [These indefinite pronouns were already discussed in reference to subject-verb agreement in Chapter 4.]

These indefinite pronouns are always singular: *each, either, neither, one*, and all that end in *–one* or *–body* (*anyone, everyone, no one, someone, anybody, everybody, nobody,* and *somebody*).

> *Each* of the students brought *their* own protractor to class. (incorrect)
> *Each* of the students brought *his* own protractor to class. (correct)

These indefinite pronouns are always plural: *both, few, several, many*.

> *Several* of the books were missing *its* cover. (incorrect)
> *Several* of the books were missing *their* covers. (correct)

Some indefinite pronouns are sometimes singular and sometimes plural, depending on their use in the sentence. They are *some, any, none, all,* and *most*. They frequently are followed by prepositional phrases which indicate whether they should be understood as singular or plural. If you can count the items in the prepositional phrase, the pronoun is plural; if not, it is singular.

> *All* of the information could be traced back to *its* source. (singular)
> *All* of the witnesses refused to give *their* testimony voluntarily. (plural)

If the antecedent of a pronoun consists of two (or more) singular antecedents joined by *and*, use a plural pronoun.

> *Arlene and Louise* frequently donate *their* time to the Manna Food Bank.

If the antecedent of a pronoun consists of two (or more) singular antecedents joined by *or* or *nor,* use a singular pronoun.

> *Neither Huck Finn nor his friend* Tom Sawyer revealed *his* actual identity to Aunt Sally.

If the antecedent of a pronoun consists of two (or more) plural antecedents (whether joined by *and* or by *or* or *nor*), use a plural pronoun.

> *Both the teachers and the students* gave *their* opinions on the questionnaire.
> *Neither the teachers nor the students* gave *their* opinions on the questionnaire.

If the antecedent of a pronoun consists of two (or more) antecedents joined by *or* or *nor*, and one of them is singular and one of them is plural, make the pronoun agree with the antecedent nearer to it.

> *Neither Dr. Martin nor the history professors* have given *their* opinion of the new proposal.
> *Neither the history professors nor Dr. Martin* has given *his* opinion of the new proposal.

A relative pronoun (like *who, which*, and *that*) used as the subject of a dependent clause has the same number as its antecedent.

> Rachel is a person *who* is willing to give *her* time to help others. (The antecedent of *who* is the singular noun *person*, so the pronoun is singular.)
> Rachel and Jason are people *who* are willing to give *their* time to help others. (The antecedent of *who* is the plural noun *people*, so the pronoun is plural.)

A pronoun must agree with its antecedent in gender. Gender is the quality of being masculine (male), feminine (female), or neuter (neither).

The third person singular personal pronouns (*he, him, his, she, her, hers, it, its*) are the only personal pronouns that refer to particular genders. Of course, *he, him*, and *his* are masculine; *she, her*, and *hers* are feminine; and *it* and *its* are neuter.

> Considering *his* small salary, *Bob Cratchitt* provided the best *he* could for *his* family.
> *Queen Elizabeth* often went on trips called "progresses" around *her* kingdom in order to become better known to *her* subjects.
> A *tree* reveals *its* age in the number of *its* growth rings.

If the antecedent is an animal and the gender of the animal is known, make the pronoun agree with the correct gender. If the gender is unknown, you may use a neuter pronoun.

> *The sow* was followed by *her* eight piglets.
> *The bull* tossed *his* head from side to side.
> *A giraffe* has seven bones in *its* neck, just like a mouse.

If the antecedent is an animal the gender of which is unknown and you wish to call special attention to the animal, you may use a masculine pronoun.

> The old man's *dog* refused to leave *his* master, no matter what.

Some difficulty is presented when a pronoun refers to a person and the gender of the person is unknown or when a pronoun refers to a group composed of both males and females. Traditionally, in English and in other languages, such instances have been called "common gender," and the masculine pronoun has been used.

> *Somebody* has left *his* umbrella.
> *Each* of the authors gave permission for *his* work to be reprinted.

Recently, some have suggested that this use of the masculine pronoun for these "common gender" situations implies a lack of sensitivity for recent changes in male and female relationships and occupations. Others have labeled it as blatant "sexism." There have been various attempts by modern writers to accommodate these non-traditional notions by using "inclusivist" language. Some have started using such phrases as "he or she," "him or her," "his or her," etc. Others have begun using "he/she," "him/her," "his/her," etc. Some have suggested that in such situations the speaker or writer should use masculine pronouns about half the time and feminine pronouns about half the time. For those who are traditionalists in culture and in language, such politically-motivated suggestions seem outlandish. On the other hand, even we traditionalists do not want to be considered ill-mannered or discourteous or intemperate, given the current rather heated climate of gender politics in some quarters. So what is a traditionalist speaker or writer to do?

You may feel free to continue to use the masculine pronoun when referring to an antecedent with common gender, remembering that this is grammatical gender—which is not the same at all necessarily as sexual gender.

> *Everyone* should turn in *his* paper at the end of class.
> *A professor* should let *his* students know the requirements of the course.

Or you may wish, in certain situations of a limited nature, to recognize the realities of modern culture by using the "he or she" formula.

> *Everyone* should turn in *his or her* paper at the end of class.
> *A professor* should let *his or her* students know the requirements of the course.

Or, in order to avoid the problem, you may make the sentence plural, if possible.

> *Students* should turn in *their papers* at the end of class.
> *Professors* should let *their* students know the requirements of *their courses*.

But a few warnings are in order:

If used repeatedly, the "he or she" method can become a quagmire and become quite awkward, both in speech and in writing.

> *Everyone* should turn in *his or her* paper as *he or she* leaves class.
> *A professor* should publish the requirements of *his or her* course in *his or her* syllabus, which *he or she* will pass out in the first class period.

The "he/she" method is ugly and smacks of officialdom. It should be avoided totally.

Finally, under absolutely no conditions should you ever use a plural pronoun to refer to a singular antecedent.

> *Everyone* should turn in *their* papers at the end of class. (incorrect)
> *A professor* should let *their* students know the requirements of the course. (incorrect)

Chapter 6

Adjectives and Adverbs and Their Usage

Distinguishing Adjectives and Adverbs

It is important to distinguish between adjectives and adverbs. You may try to distinguish between them merely by how they are spelled. You may notice that many adverbs end in *–ly* (*slyly, loudly, rudely*). However, there are adverbs that do not end in *–ly* (*soon, often, well*), and there are adjectives that do end in *–ly* (*godly, early, friendly*). The best way to distinguish between adjectives and adverbs is by their function. Use adjectives to modify nouns and pronouns. Use adverbs to modify verbs, adjectives, and adverbs.

> The children behaved improper. (incorrect—the adjective *improper* is modifying the verb *behaved*)
> The children behaved *improperly*. (correct—the adverb *improperly* is modifying the verb *behaved*)

One very common error is to use an adverb after a linking verb to modify the subject. Rather, you should use a predicate adjective.

> I now feel *differently* about those events. (incorrect)
> I now feel *different* about those events. (correct)

Comparison

Adjectives and adverbs are said to have three degrees of comparison: positive, comparative, and superlative.

The positive degree is used when no comparison is being expressed.

adjectives

> The pine tree is *tall*.
> He is a *helpful* clerk.
> That was an *insightful* question.

adverbs

The troops stood *firm*.
They walked down the road *slowly*.
She answered *rapidly*.

The comparative degree is used to compare only two things.

adjectives

The pine tree is *taller* than the oak generally.
He is *more helpful* than the other clerks.
His second question was *more insightful* than his first.

adverbs

The British troops stood *more firmly* than the French troops.
They walked *more slowly* than they had done earlier.
She answered *more rapidly* than the others.

The superlative degree is used to compare three or more things.

adjectives

The pine tree is the *tallest* tree in the garden.
Of all the clerks, he is the *most helpful*.
That was the *most insightful* question of the whole class period.

adverbs

Of all the troops, this battalion stood the *most firmly*.
The old man walked along *most slowly* of all, bringing up the end of the long line of mourners.
Evelyn answered *most rapidly* of all the contestants.

Most one-syllable adjectives and adverbs form their comparative and superlative degrees by adding *–er* and *–est*.

positive	**comparative**	**superlative**
big	bigger	biggest
strong	stronger	strongest

Most two-syllable adjectives and adverbs form their comparative and superlative degrees by adding *more* and *most*.

positive	**comparative**	**superlative**
eager	more eager	most eager
honest	more honest	most honest
quickly	more quickly	most quickly

A few two-syllable adjectives and adverbs form their comparative and superlative degrees by adding *–er* and *–est*. When in doubt, look them up in a dictionary.

positive	**comparative**	**superlative**
happy	happier	happiest
noble	nobler	noblest

Adjectives and adverbs of three or more syllables form their comparative and superlative degrees by adding *more* and *most*.

positive	**comparative**	**superlative**
reliable	more reliable	most reliable
gorgeously	more gorgeously	most gorgeously

Some adjectives and adverbs do not use these regular methods of comparison and form their comparative and superlative forms irregularly.

positive	**comparative**	**superlative**
good/well	better	best
little	less	least
much/many	more	most

To indicate less or least of a quality, use the words *less* or *least* in the comparison.

positive	**comparative**	**superlative**
thick	less thick	least thick
happy	less happy	least happy
magnificently	less magnificently	least magnificently

Usage

Use the comparative degree for comparing two things and the superlative degree for comparing three or more things.

Which of the two songs seems to fit into the program *better*?
Bob is the *shortest* of the three boys on the back row.

Do not use double comparison. Use either *–er*/*–est* or *more*/*most*, not both together.

Is this board *more longer* than that one? (incorrect)
Is this board *longer* than that one? (correct)

After lunch, we worked *more slowlier*. (incorrect)
After lunch, we worked *more slowly*. (correct)

Use *other* or *else* when comparing a thing with a group of which it is a part.

After the Cold War, the United States was stronger militarily than any country in the world. (incorrect—the United States cannot be stronger than itself)
After the Cold War, the United States was stronger militarily than any *other* country in the world. (correct)

My sister Martha sings better than anyone in her family. (incorrect—Martha cannot sing better than herself)
My sister Martha sings better than anyone *else* in her family. (correct)

Though one is tempted to think that, if one negative word is good, then two or more negative words are better, unfortunately, this useful (and once widely used and accepted) idiomatic expression is no longer used. Hence, do not use the double negative. Negative words include the following: *not* (or *n't*), *never, none, no one, nothing, hardly, scarcely*, and *but* (when it means "only").

We do*n't* have *no* more potatoes. (incorrect)
We do*n't* have *any* more potatoes. (correct)
We have *no* more potatoes. (correct)

At that point of the war, the Colonies did *not scarcely* have three experienced generals. (incorrect)
At that point of the war, the Colonies *scarcely* had three experienced generals. (correct)
At that point of the war, the Colonies did *not* have three experienced generals. (correct)

Chapter 7
Sentence Composition

Composition begins, not with the writing of poetry or fiction or essays, not even with the writing of good paragraphs, though they are crucial for good writing. Rather, it begins with the writing of good sentences. Henry David Thoreau—though wrong on many things—was right when he said, "A sentence should read as if its author, had he held a plow instead of a pen, could have drawn a furrow deep and straight to the end." In this book we have so far looked at the structure of the English sentence and at the main parts of speech and their usage. Now we turn to sentence composition. Effective sentences are complete, well constructed, and clear.

Sentences, Fragments, and Run-ons

A sentence is a group of words that expresses a complete thought and can stand alone. A sentence will have a verb and a subject (either expressed or understood) and may have complements. It may certainly contain phrases or clauses which modify the verb, subject, or complements or which are actually used as a subject or complement themselves.

A fragment, however, is only part of a sentence. It may be a phrase (such as a prepositional phrase, a participial phrase, a gerund phrase, an infinitive phrase, an appositive phrase, or a nominative absolute), or it may be a clause (with a subject and a verb—an adjective clause, a noun clause, or an adverb clause). Even if it has a subject and verb it is not a sentence unless it expresses a complete thought and can stand alone.

Ophelia did not know what to think. *Because of Hamlet's strange behavior.* (prepositional phrase)
Chaucer's Wife of Bath is on her way to Canterbury. *To find herself another husband.* (infinitive phrase)
The pilgrims were going to Canterbury. *The shrine of St. Thomas á Beckett.* (appositive phrase)
Polonius manipulated his daughter. *So that he could get information about Hamlet.* (adverb clause)

Romeo and Juliet being members of feuding families. They kept their betrothal secret. (nominative absolute)

A fragment may simply need to be reconnected to a sentence from which it has become separated.

Because of Hamlet's strange behavior, Ophelia did not know what to think.
Chaucer's Wife of Bath is on her way to Canterbury *to find herself another husband.*
The pilgrims were going to Canterbury, *the shrine of St. Thomas á Beckett.*
Polonius manipulated his daughter *so that he could get information about Hamlet.*
Romeo and Juliet being members of feuding families, they kept their betrothal secret.

Sometimes, however, the fragment will need to be rewritten. You may need to add words or delete words to make the fragment into a complete sentence.

The modern necktie, which is a descendant of the cravat. (fragment)
The modern necktie is a descendant of the cravat. (sentence)

A run-on sentence is the opposite of a fragment. It is two or more sentences which have been erroneously joined together and written as one sentence. Two independent clauses may become a run-on when they are simply joined together with no punctuation at all. They may become a run-on when they are joined together with only a comma. This latter form of run-on is sometimes called a "comma splice." Two independent clauses can be correctly joined together only by means of a comma and a coordinating conjunction (*and, but, or, nor, for, yet, so*) or by means of a semicolon.

The American Revolution began at Lexington in 1775, it ended at Yorktown in 1781. (incorrect—a comma splice)
The American Revolution began at Lexington it ended at Yorktown. (incorrect—no comma and coordinating conjunction)

A run-on sentence can be corrected several ways.

You may separate the two parts into separate sentences.

The American Revolution began at Lexington in 1775. It ended at Yorktown in 1781.

You may correct it through coordination (joining things together as equals), using either a comma and a coordinating conjunction or a semicolon.

The American Revolution began at Lexington in 1775, and it ended at Yorktown in 1781.
The American Revolution began at Lexington in 1775; it ended at Yorktown in 1781.

You may correct it through subordination (joining things together as unequals). Turn one of the parts into a phrase or a dependent clause.

The American Revolution, *begun at Lexington in 1775*, finally came to an end at Yorktown in 1781. (participial phrase)
The American Revolution, *which began at Lexington in 1775*, finally came to an end at Yorktown in 1781. (adjective clause)

Coordination

Excessive coordination produces two problems. A string of independent clauses joined by *and* or *so* can be boring to the reader. Coordination is also rather imprecise; it does not always express the exact relationship of ideas adequately. If a sentence uses too much coordination, break it up into separate sentences or make some of the independent clauses into phrases or dependent clauses.

They were in the museum, and they purchased several art prints.
While they were in the museum, they purchased several art prints.

Emily was not feeling well, so she went home early.
Since Emily was not feeling well, she went home early.

Elizabeth Bennet is the heroine of *Pride and Prejudice*, and she overcomes her prejudice against Mr. Darcy.
Elizabeth Bennet, the heroine of *Pride and Prejudice*, overcomes her prejudice against Mr. Darcy.

When using coordination, be sure to join things that are equal. Do not join together an independent clause and a dependent clause with a coordinating conjunction.

Monticello is a beautiful home and which is built in the classical style.
Monticello is a beautiful home which is built in the classical style.

Subordination

The proper use of subordination is the mark of a good writer. Take ideas that are of lesser importance and subordinate them to ideas that are of greater importance. Of course, as with coordination, you do not want to use subordination too much. A string of clauses, each modifying a word in the previous one, can seem contrived and artificial. It can also be quite confusing to the reader.

> They installed a new bookcase, which is made of oak, which is both strong and beautiful. (excessive subordination)

Be sure that your efforts at subordination are logical. For instance, do not use an adverb clause as a predicate nominative or other noun.

> The reason Parliament rebelled was because Charles I had acted unconstitutionally. (incorrect)
> The reason Parliament rebelled was that Charles I had acted unconstitutionally. (correct)
> Parliament rebelled because Charles I had acted unconstitutionally. (correct)

Likewise, do not use an independent clause as a noun.

> The immediate cause of World War II was Germany invaded Poland. (incorrect)
> The immediate cause of World War II was that Germany invaded Poland. (correct)
> The immediate cause of World War II was Germany's invasion of Poland. (correct)

Misplaced Modifiers

Modifiers (whether adjectives or adverbs, adjective or adverb prepositional phrases, participial phrases, infinitive phrases, or adjective or adverb clauses) should generally be placed as near as possible to the words they modify. Placement elsewhere can affect the meaning of the sentence. Correct misplaced modifiers simply by moving them within the sentence.

> *Only* Margie washed the dishes.
> Margie *only* washed the dishes.
> Margie washed *only* the dishes.

> The emigrants *from Appalachia* carried language and customs with them on their trek.

The emigrants carried language and customs *from Appalachia* with them on their trek.
The emigrants carried language and customs with them on their trek *from Appalachia*.

Lying under the sofa, he found his notebook.
He found his notebook *lying under the sofa*.

Placement of a modifier in such a position that it may seem to modify more than one word will cause confusion. Such modifiers are sometimes called "squinting modifiers."

Mrs. DeMerchant said *on Friday* we would have a test on punctuation. (incorrect)
On Friday, Mrs. DeMerchant said we would have a test on punctuation. (correct)
Mrs. DeMerchant said we would have a test on punctuation *on Friday*. (correct)

Be careful not to split infinitives or parts of verb phrases unnecessarily.

Jenna *had* for some time *been planning* a trip to Mexico. (incorrect)
Jenna *had been planning* a trip to Mexico for some time. (correct)

The director reminded us *to* clearly and slowly *speak our lines*. (incorrect)
The director reminded us *to speak our lines* clearly and slowly. (correct)

Of course, this does not mean that infinitives or verb phrases should never be split. Sometimes adverbs occur quite naturally within infinitives or verb phrases, and to place them elsewhere would make the sentence more awkward.

Totally to eliminate the income tax is certainly our goal. (incorrect)
To totally eliminate the income tax is certainly our goal. (correct)

Dangling Modifiers

Some problem modifiers cannot be corrected merely by being moved because they have nothing to modify. These are called "dangling modifiers." To correct these you will need to rewrite the sentence, perhaps even supplying additional information.

Sitting on the back row, the choir could barely be heard. (dangling)
Sitting on the back row, we could barely hear the choir. (correct)

While running in the marathon, a cramp developed in James's left leg. (incorrect)
While running in the marathon, James developed a cramp in his left leg. (correct)

To learn Latin, the different verb conjugations must be mastered. (dangling)
To learn Latin, you must master the different verb conjugations. (correct)

At the age of three, his family moved to Indiana. (dangling)
His family moved to Indiana when he was three years old. (correct)

When asked about this, no answer was given. (dangling)
When asked about this, the attorney general gave no answer. (correct)

Some phrases, though technically dangling, have become so commonly used that they are clearly understood and accepted.

Considering his poor education, he was remarkably well read.
The project should proceed, *provided there is sufficient funding available*.

Pronoun Reference

Every pronoun must have a clear antecedent (a noun or pronoun to which it refers).

Pronouns have ambiguous reference when there seem to be two or more possible antecedents. To correct ambiguous reference, either replace the pronoun with its antecedent or rewrite the sentence.

Erica called Carol several times while she was sick. (antecedent of *she* is ambiguous)
While Erica was sick, she called Carol several times. (clear)
While Carol was sick, Erica called her several times. (clear)

The workers in the stock room removed the cans from the boxes and stacked them in the corner. (antecedent of *them* is ambiguous)
The workers in the stock room removed the cans from the boxes and stacked the cans in the corner. (clear)
The workers in the stock room removed the cans from the boxes and stacked the boxes in the corner. (clear)

Pronouns have implied reference when the antecedent is not actually present but is merely implied. Such sentences tend to be vague and imprecise. To correct implied reference, replace the unclear pronoun with a noun.

> He has written some poetry, but none of them have been published. (antecedent of *them* is only implied)
> He has written some poetry, but none of his poems have been published. (clear)

> Yes, the boys fished all day, but they didn't catch any. (antecedent of *any* is only implied)
> Yes, the boys fished all day, but they didn't catch any fish at all. (clear)

Pronouns have broad reference when they refer to an entire clause rather than to a particular noun or pronoun antecedent. To correct broad reference, either supply a necessary antecedent or rewrite the sentence.

> During class, Dave cracked his knuckles several times, which annoyed everyone. (what is the antecedent of *which*?)
> During class, Dave annoyed everyone by cracking his knuckles several times. (clear)

> We need to make sure that there is a lifeguard on duty at all times, even if it does cost more money. (what is the antecedent of *it*?)
> Even if keeping a lifeguard on duty at all times costs more money, we should do it. (clear)

Take care not to use the pronouns *it, you*, and *they* indefinitely. Either supply the pronoun with a clear antecedent or rewrite the sentence.

> In Washington *they* do not seem to understand the farm crisis. (indefinite—who are *they*?)
> The politicians in Washington do not seem to understand the farm crisis. (clear)

> In today's paper, *it* says that the councilman has been indicted. (indefinite—what is *it*?)
> Today's paper says that the councilman has been indicted. (clear)

> In a totalitarian country, *you* are controlled from the cradle to the grave. (indefinite—who is *you*?)
> In a totalitarian country, the people are controlled from the cradle to the grave. (clear)

The pronoun *you* may, of course, properly refer to the reader. In some types of formal writing, however, you will probably want to avoid this usage.

Parallelism

Just as lines in geometry may be parallel if they do not intersect, grammatical forms are said to be parallel if they are alike structurally. Using two or more similar grammatical forms together will give your writing strength and balance. However, if you should introduce an element which does not fit, the result will be awkwardness and imbalance.

> In the elementary grades children should learn [fractions] and [how to do long division]. (not parallel)
> In the elementary grades children should learn [fractions] and [long division]. (parallel)

> Our accountants urged [us to raise prices] and [that we reduce costs as much as possible]. (not parallel)
> Our accountants urged [that we raise prices] and [that we lower costs]. (parallel)
> Our accountants urged us [to raise prices] and [to lower costs]. (parallel)
> Our accountants urged us to [raise prices] and [lower costs]. (parallel)

> Tolkien's novels contain [fantastic characters] but [which have realistic human emotions]. (not parallel)
> Tolkien's novels contain characters [which are fantastic] but [which have realistic human emotions]. (parallelism improved)
> Tolkien's novels contain fantastic characters with realistic human emotions. (parallelism removed)

Be especially careful to achieve parallelism when you are using correlative conjunctions (conjunctions which come in pairs): *either ... or, neither ... nor, both ... and, not only ... but also*. Each part of these sets should come immediately in front of the parallel elements.

> The remote village could be reached *either* [on foot] *or* [you could fly in]. (not parallel)
> The remote village could be reached *either* [on foot] *or* [by plane]. (parallel)

> *Both* [in Columbia] *and* [Mexico], there is significant drug smuggling. (not parallel)

Both [in Columbia] *and* [in Mexico], there is significant drug smuggling. (parallel)
In *both* [Columbia] *and* [Mexico], there is significant drug smuggling. (parallel)

Sometimes, in order to achieve clarity in parallelism, you may need to repeat necessary words.

The terrain of the battlefield was a greater problem [for the English] than [the Scots]. (Perhaps the terrain was a greater problem for the English than the Scots were.)
The terrain of the battlefield was a greater problem [for the English] than [for the Scots]. (The terrain was more of a problem for the English than it was for the Scots.)

Of course, in this as in all things, appropriateness and moderation is the key. By insisting on absolute parallelism you may make the sentence more awkward and more imbalanced.

Stephen addressed the Sanhedrin [powerfully] and [with great conviction]. (True, *powerfully* is an adverb and *with great conviction* is a prepositional phrase. But both are used as adverbs, and there is no single adverb in English meaning "with great conviction.")

Clarity and Logic

To achieve clarity and logic in your writing, do not make logical "leaps."

For instance, do not leave out necessary words.

His proposal was as good, if not better than mine. (unclear)
His proposal was as good *as*, if not better than mine. (clear)

The explorers were going where no one ever had before. (unclear)
The explorers were going where no one ever had *gone* before. (clear)

We must be able to have respect and confidence in our leaders. (unclear)
We must be able to have respect *for* and confidence in our leaders. (clear)

Also, do not use non sequiturs. The Latin expression *non sequitur* literally means "it does not follow." A non sequitur is an introductory phrase or clause which really has no logical connection with the rest of the sentence. You will find these frequently in the world of journalism. Journalism students may be encouraged to put as much information as possible into the opening sentence or two in an article. Unfortunately, like some other practices in journalism these days, this suggestion may lead to increased confusion and illogic.

> *Born in Stratford in 1564*, Shakespeare became the most famous English playwright of all time. (What does "born in Stratford in 1564" have to do with Shakespeare's becoming the most famous English playwright of all time? Surely there were others born in Stratford in 1564 who did not become famous playwrights. Non sequitur—it does not follow.)
>
> *Though born in the small town of Stratford far from the centers of learning and literature*, Shakespeare nevertheless became the most famous English playwright of all time. (Now the opening phrase is logically connected with the rest of the sentence. Sequitur—it follows.)
>
> *Born in 1564*, Shakespeare was only about twenty-five years old when his first play, *Titus Andronicus*, was produced, perhaps in 1589. (This opening phrase is also logically connected with the rest of the sentence. Sequitur—it follows.)

Unnecessary Shifts

Unnecessary shifts may create confusion.

For instance, do not shift unnecessarily in verb tense, mood, or voice.

> During the course of the play, Gloucester *comes* to realize that he is a sinner and has made huge errors of judgment. He also *realized* that human life is a divine gift. (The writer has shifted unnecessarily from the present tense verb *comes* to the past tense verb *realized*.)
>
> During the course of the play, Gloucester *comes* to realize that he is a sinner and has made huge errors of judgment. He also *realizes* that human life is a divine gift. (correct)
>
> If I *were* you and *was* in your situation, I would try to find a new job. (The writer has shifted unnecessarily from the subjunctive mood verb *were* to the indicative mood verb *was*.)
> If I *were* you and *were* in your situation, I would try to find a new job. (correct)

My grandfather *did* not *leave* his family a great deal of money, but a heritage of integrity and charity *was bequeathed* to them. (The writer has shifted unnecessarily from the active voice verb *did leave* to the passive voice verb *was bequeathed*.)

My grandfather *did* not *leave* his family a great deal of money, but he *did bequeath* them a heritage of integrity and charity. (correct)

Do not shift unnecessarily in the person and number of nouns and pronouns.

If *a person* will pay attention in class and do the homework exercises, *you* will find that learning a foreign language is not that difficult. (The writer has shifted unnecessarily from the third person subject *a person* to the second person subject *you*.)
If *a person* will pay attention in class and do the homework exercises, *he* will find that learning a foreign language is not that difficult. (correct)
The faculty *invites* graduates and their families to join *them* for the annual graduate reception. (The writer has shifted unnecessarily from referring to the faculty as singular—as seen in the singular verb *invites*—to referring to the faculty as plural—as seen in the plural pronoun *them*.)
The faculty *invite* the graduates and their families to join *them* for the annual graduate reception. (correct)

Direct discourse uses the exact words of someone. Indirect discourse gives a summary of another's words. Do not shift unnecessarily between these two types of statement.

The receptionist *said that Dr. Ketteman was out of the office* and *would I like to leave a message*. (The writer has shifted unnecessarily from indirect discourse to direct discourse.)
The receptionist *said that Dr. Ketteman was out of the office* and *asked if I would like to leave a message*. (correct)

Do not shift the tone or style unnecessarily.

The incessant moaning of the wind, the creaking of the limbs overhead, and the impenetrable darkness *gave me the creeps*. (The writer has shifted unnecessarily from a very formal tone to a very informal tone.)
The incessant moaning of the wind, the creaking of the limbs overhead, and the impenetrable darkness *gave me a definite sense of foreboding*. (correct)

Do not shift subjects unnecessarily.

> *Herbert's poetry* can be quite challenging; sometimes *I* cannot understand his imagery. (The writer has shifted the subject from Herbert's poetry to himself.)
>
> *Herbert's poetry* can be quite challenging; sometimes *his imagery* can be difficult to understand. (correct)

Chapter 8
Sentence Diagraming

By the end of the nineteenth century, modernism in its various forms was beginning to effect huge changes in the teaching of English grammar. At first it was the so-called "progressives," who were, in effect, ending the traditional study of grammar, insisting that it had little connection with "real life." Then modern linguistics, with its foundation in Darwinism, turned its attention away from the examination of language and literature per se to research into the human mind and how it "generates" language. Such a speculative study may have some merits (were it not approached from rigidly materialist Darwinian presuppositions and were it not intimately connected with the rejection of theism and the entire secularist/modernist agenda). However, such speculations are certainly not the same thing as instruction in grammar. The entire impetus behind modern linguistics is, in fact, the attempt to turn all concepts connected with language into "scientific" ones (i.e., concepts based merely and solely upon empirical data). It is a rejection of the concept of *a priori* or innate ideas resulting from a supernatural origin.

Oddly, it was about this time that one of the last genuine developments in traditional grammar appeared. In 1849 in his book *Practical Grammar Illustrated by a Complete System of Diagrams*, Stephen Clark introduced a method of diagraming sentences. The system he developed was an excellent attempt to help students in traditional grammar classrooms to show on paper the sentence parsing that had been a staple of grammar for over two millennia. A few years later, in 1875, two English professors at the Brooklyn Collegiate and Polytechnic Institute (now called Polytechnic University) by the very Victorian names of Alonzo Reed and Brainerd Kellogg refined Clark's diagrams further. Whereas Clark had used a series of "balloons" to indicate clauses and phrases, Reed and Kellogg used a series of lines, indicating the relationships of the various parts of the sentence. They proceeded to write two English grammar textbooks: *Graded Lessons in English* (1875) and *Higher Lessons in English* (1878). Reacting against those grammars with long lists of rules to memorize, Reed and Kellogg "used an inductive approach, presenting concepts with a minimum of explanation, giving students many sample sentences to analyze."[1] Using horizontal, vertical, and angled lines, they were able to produce diagrams that were simple but not simplistic. These diagrams could display all the parts of the sentence clearly and elegantly.

In the second half of the twentieth century, under the influence first of structuralism and then transformational-generative grammar, sentence diagraming was generally abandoned. Some of the last traditionalist grammar textbooks to continue teaching the Reed and Kellogg diagraming method were those produced by John E. Warriner and his colleagues and published by Harcourt, Brace, and World. In some ways Warriner's grammar and composition textbooks (first published in 1948) were a rejection of progressive education and its rather vague social emphases.

The method of sentence analysis and diagraming developed by Reed and Kellogg and taught by Warriner and others was not designed, obviously, to be an end in itself. A study of syntax (especially one accompanied by sentence diagraming) would develop the language and literary skills of the student. By studying the sentence, the student would develop various intellectual and practical skills.

Reed and Kellogg's commitment to the study of the sentence is paramount to their method. In the preface to their *Higher Lessons in English* they assert:

> Through the study of the sentence we not only arrive at an intelligent knowledge of the parts of speech and a correct use of grammatical forms, but we discover the laws of discourse in general. In the sentence the student should find the law of unity, of continuity, of proportion, of order. All good writing consists of good sentences properly joined. Since the sentence is the foundation or unit of discourse, it is all-important that the pupil should know the sentence. He should be able to put the principal and the subordinate parts in their proper relation; he should know the exact function of every element, its relation to other elements and its relation to the whole.[2]

They saw this understanding of syntax as necessary for study of other languages as well. "The laws of thought being the same for all nations, the

[1] David Mulroy, *The War against Grammar* (Portsmouth, NH: Boynton/Cook, 2003), 89.

[2] Alonzo Reed and Brainerd Kellogg, *Higher Lessons in English, Revised Edition* (NY: Charles E. Merrill Co., 1909), iv.

logical analysis of the sentence is the same for all languages. When a student who has acquired a knowledge of the English sentence comes to the translation of a foreign language, he finds his work greatly simplified. If in a sentence of his own language he sees only a mass of unorganized words, how much greater must be his confusion when the mass of words is in a foreign tongue!"[3]

Sentence analysis was valuable for the development of the intellect. Reed and Kellogg declare:

> As a means of discipline nothing can compare with a training in the logical analysis of the sentence. To study thought through its outward form, the sentence, and to discover the fitness of the different parts of the expression to the parts of the thought is to learn to think. It has been noticed that pupils thoroughly trained in the analysis and the construction of sentences come to their other studies with a decided advantage in mental power. These results can be obtained only by systematic and persistent work. Experienced teachers understand that a few weak lessons on the sentence at the beginning of a course and a few at the end can afford little discipline and little knowledge that will endure, nor can a knowledge of the sentence be gained by memorizing complicated rules and labored forms of analysis.

It is for this detailed understanding of the sentence that they developed their sentence diagrams.

> In written analysis, the simple map, or diagram, ... will enable the pupil to present directly and vividly to the eye the exact function of every clause in the sentence, of every phrase in the clause, and of every word in the phrase—to picture the complete analysis of the sentence, with principal and subordinate parts in their proper relations. It is only by the aid of such a map, or picture, that the pupil can, at a single view, see the sentence as an organic whole made up of many parts performing various functions and standing in various relations. Without such map he must labor under the disadvantage of seeing all these things by piecemeal or in succession.[4]

Reed and Kellogg recognized that sentence diagraming was not embraced by all. Some had noted that "the pictorial diagram groups the parts of a sentence according to their offices and relations, and not in the order of speech." Some had considered this a fault. They responded: "It is, on the contrary, a merit, for

[3] Ibid., iv-v.
[4] Ibid., v-vi.

it teaches the pupil to look through the literary order and discover the logical order. He thus learns what the literary order really is, and sees that this may be varied indefinitely, so long as the logical relations are kept clear." Nor did they believe in diagraming for the sake of diagraming. "Like other good things, it is liable to be overdone," they said. "When the ordinary constructions have been made clear, diagrams should be used only for the more difficult sentences, or, if the sentences are long, only for the more difficult parts of them. ... When the diagram has served its purpose, it should be dropped."[5]

The serious student of syntax thus needs to learn and master the sentence diagram. Study these example diagrams. Notice that all sentences begin with a horizontal line crossed by a vertical line separating the subject and predicate. All other items are refinements on this Aristotelian beginning. Notice the locations of different items in the following diagrams.

Subject and Verb

King Arthur departed.

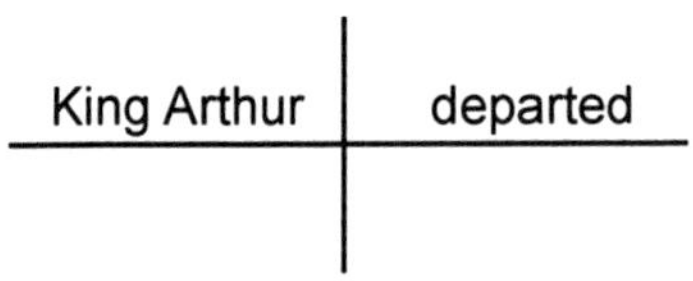

Understood Subject

Listen.

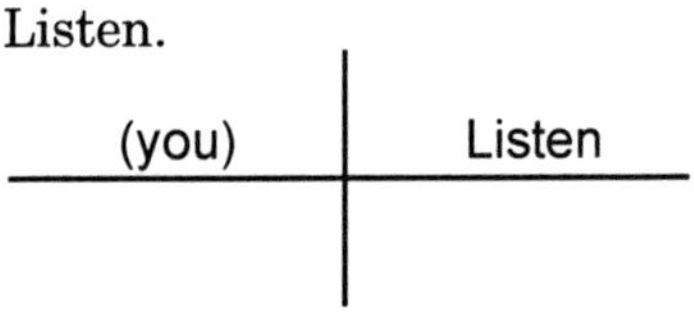

Compound Subject

Both the king and his subjects rejoiced.

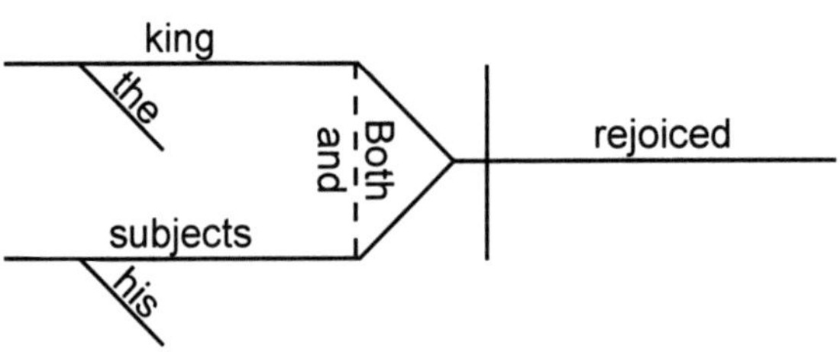

[5] Ibid., vii.

Compound Verb

He neither cared nor understood.

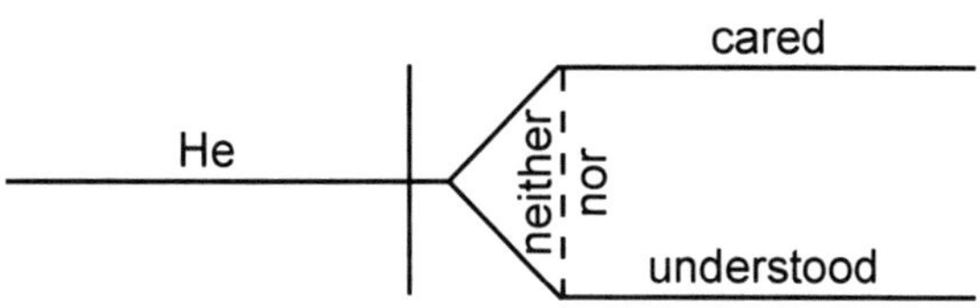

Compound Subject and Compound Verb

Rome and the empire grew and prospered.

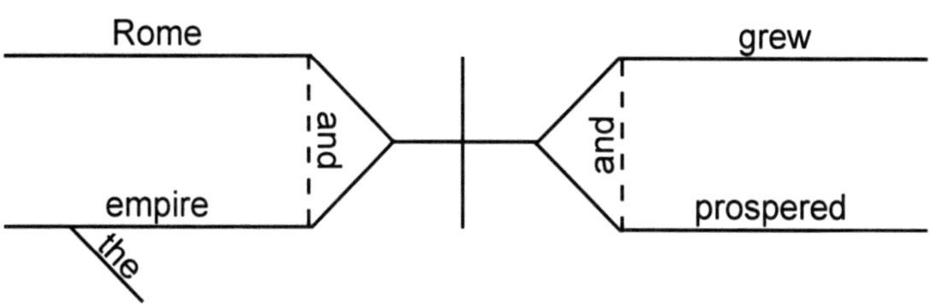

Adjective

A huge oak was uprooted.

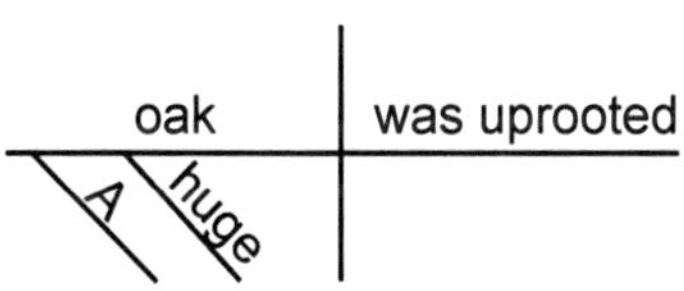

Compound Adjective

He was a poor but proud man.

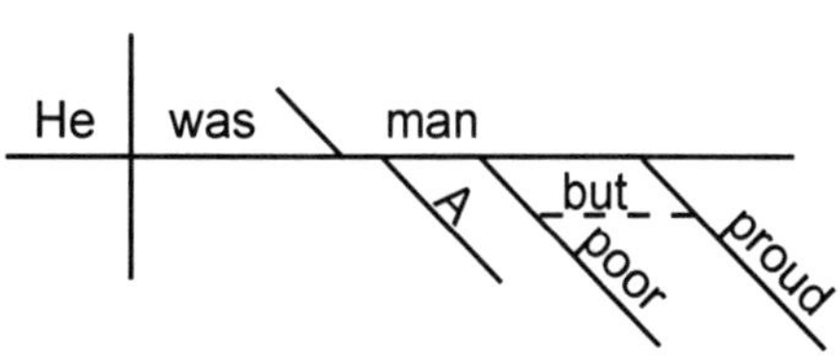

Adverb Modifying a Verb

The soldiers fought bravely.

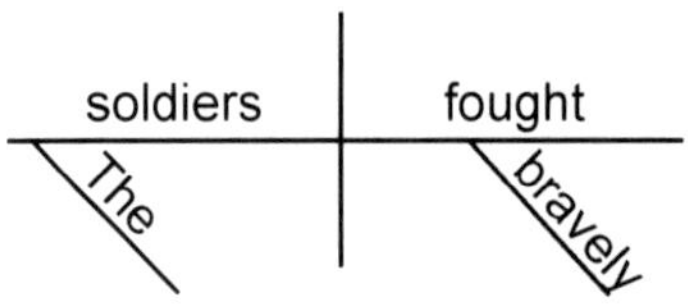

Adverb Modifying an Adjective

Why do you look so happy today?

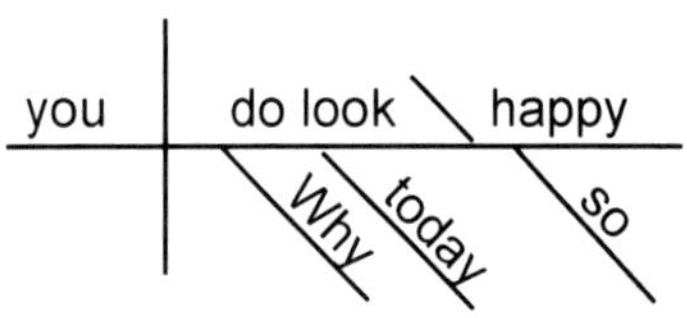

Adverb Modifying an Adverb

The gazelles fled quite suddenly.

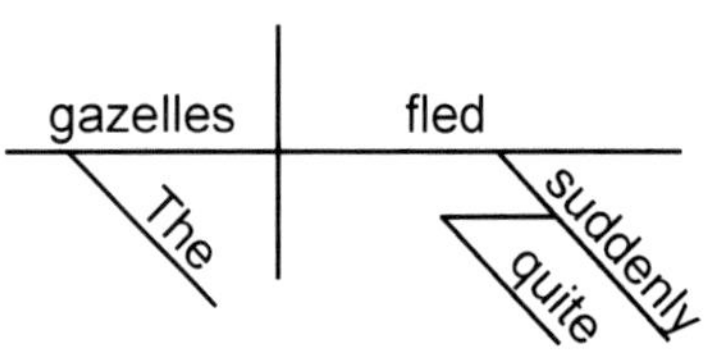

Compound Adverb

He listened carefully and thoughtfully.

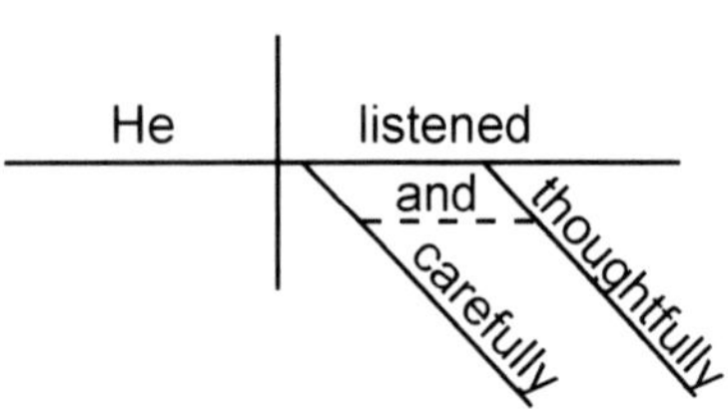

Interjection

Alas, the city is fallen!

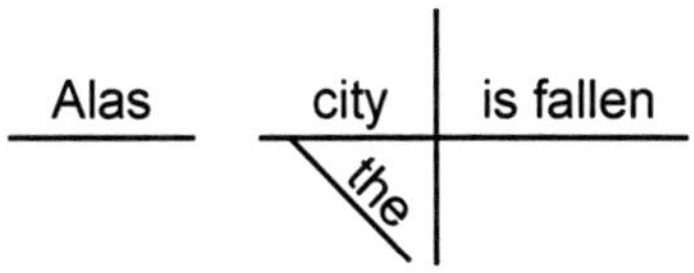

Direct Address

Kiss me, Kate. –William Shakespeare, *The Taming of the Shrew*

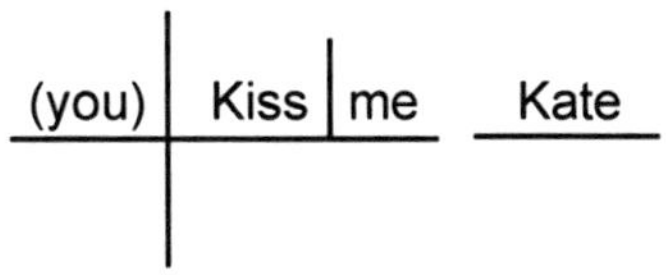

Predicate Nominative

Abraham shall surely become a great and mighty nation. –Genesis 18:18

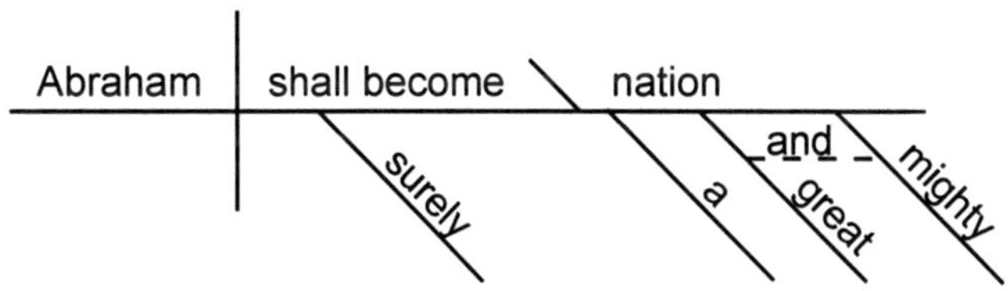

Compound Predicate Nominative

A whale ship was my Yale College and my Harvard. –Herman Melville

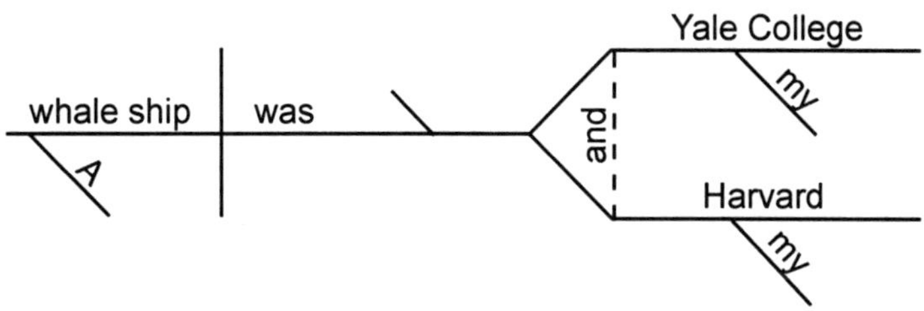

Predicate Adjective

Doomsday is near. –William Shakespeare, *1 Henry IV*

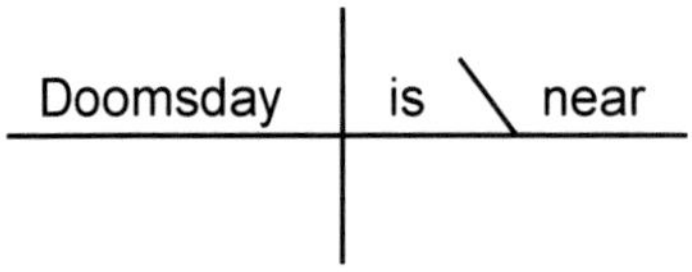

Compound Predicate Adjective

All human comfort is vain and short. –Thomas á Kempis

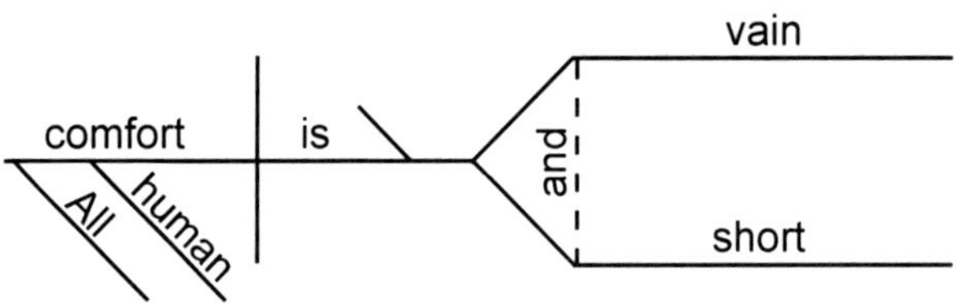

Direct Object

Faint heart never won fair lady. –William Camden

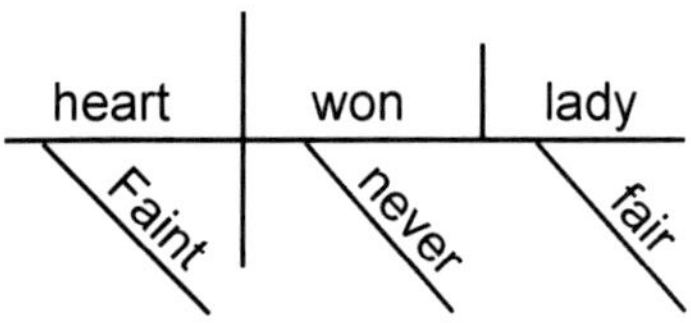

Compound Direct Object

God doth not need either man's work or His own gifts. –John Milton

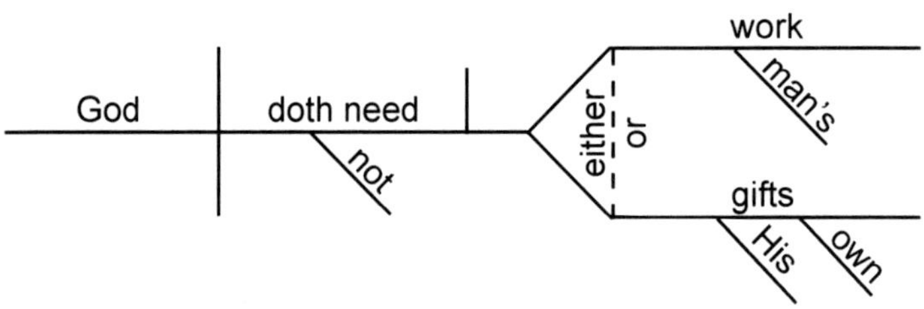

Indirect Object

Give me your hand.

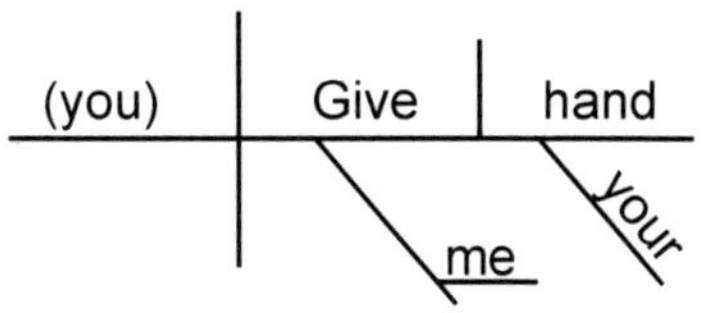

Compound Indirect Object

Lee gave Longstreet and Jackson their orders.

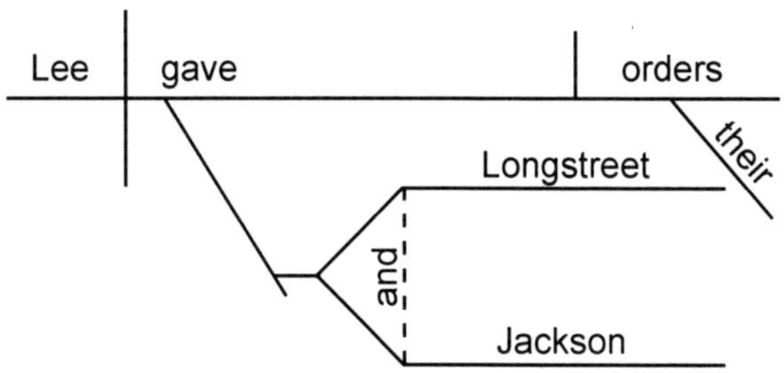

Objective Complement

Call me Ishmael. –Herman Melville

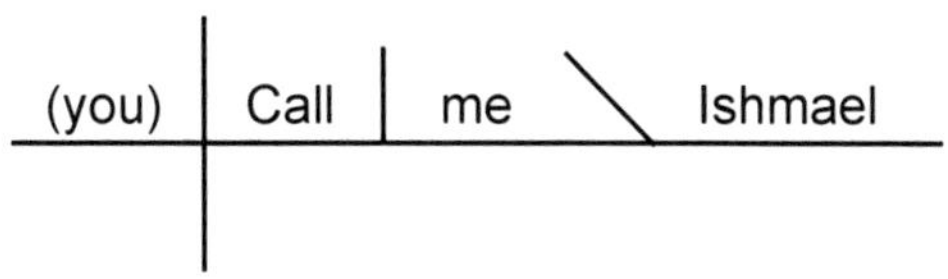

Compound Objective Complement

Ye call me Master and Lord. –John 13:13

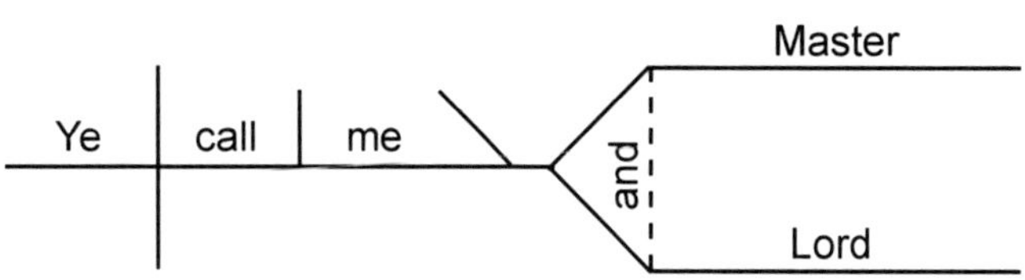

Retained Object

We were given thorough instructions.

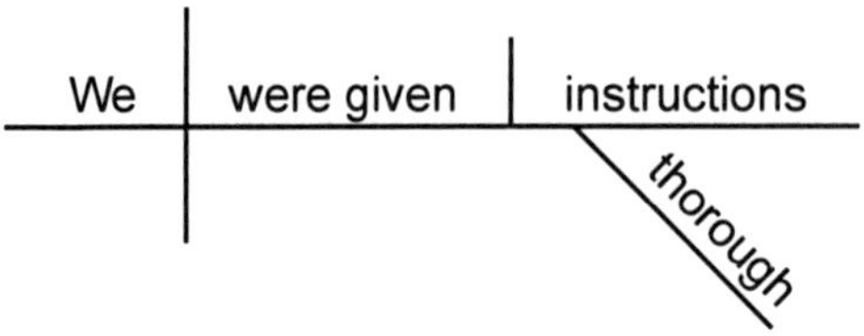

Compound Retained Object

His sons were bequeathed both his property and his good name.

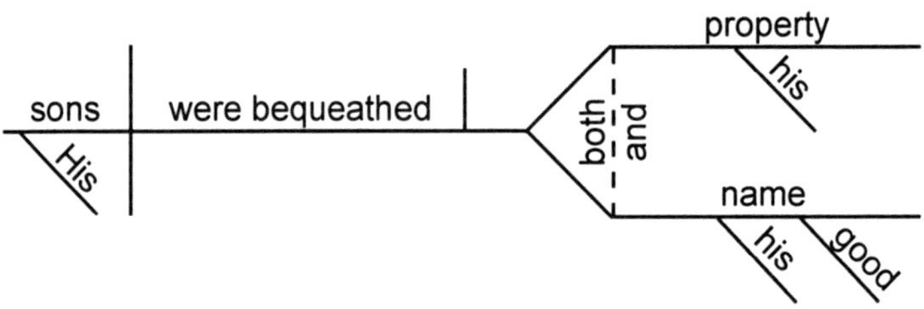

Prepositional Phrase Used as an Adjective

The young woman in this photograph is my grandmother.

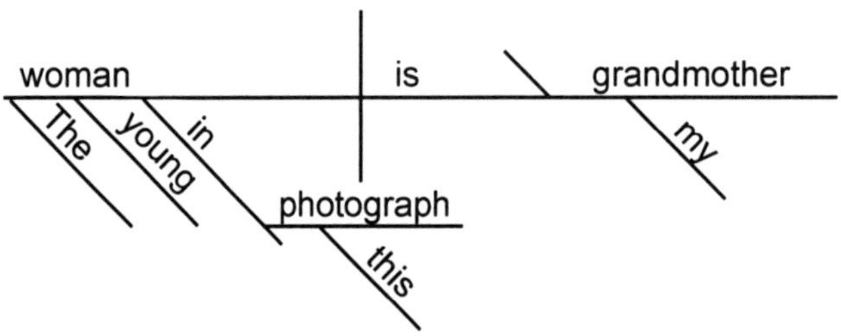

Prepositional Phrase Used as an Adverb Modifying a Verb

I cannot live without books. –Thomas Jefferson

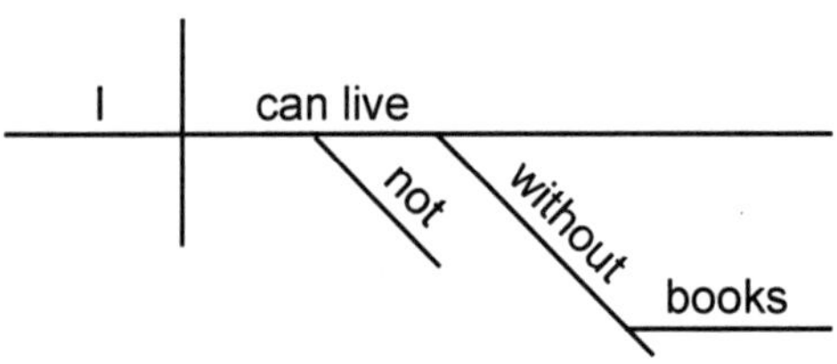

Prepositional Phrase Used as an Adverb Modifying an Adjective

Were you unsure about the outcome?

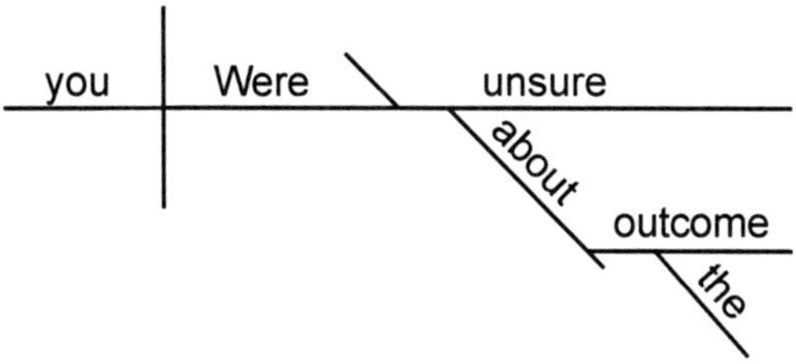

Prepositional Phrase Used as an Adverb Modifying an Adverb

They will return later in the afternoon.

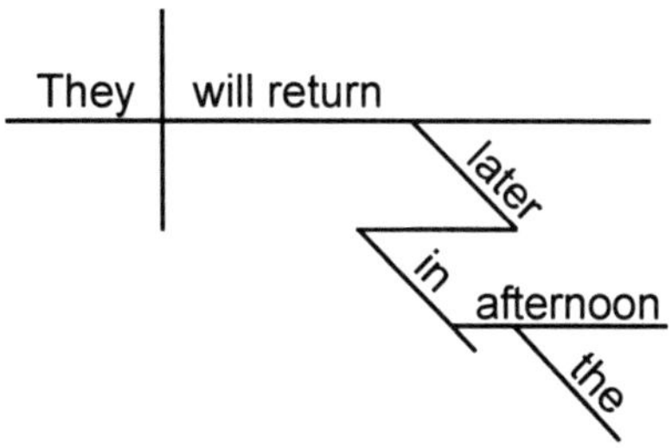

Prepositional Phrase with Compound Object

God has given the earth to man for his use and enjoyment. –John Locke

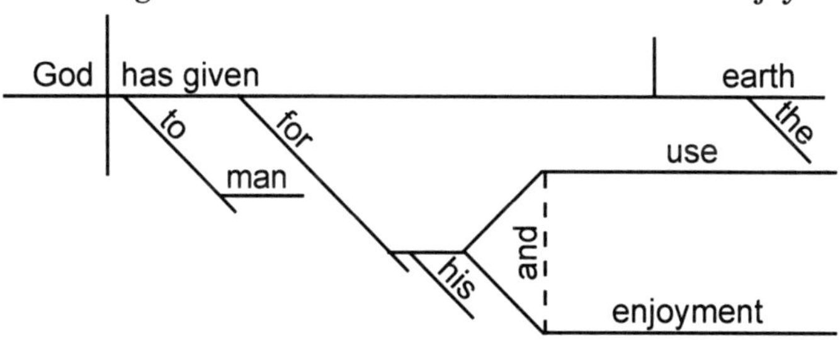

Prepositional Phrase Modifying the Object of Another Prepositional Phrase

Honesty is the first chapter in the book of wisdom. –Thomas Jefferson

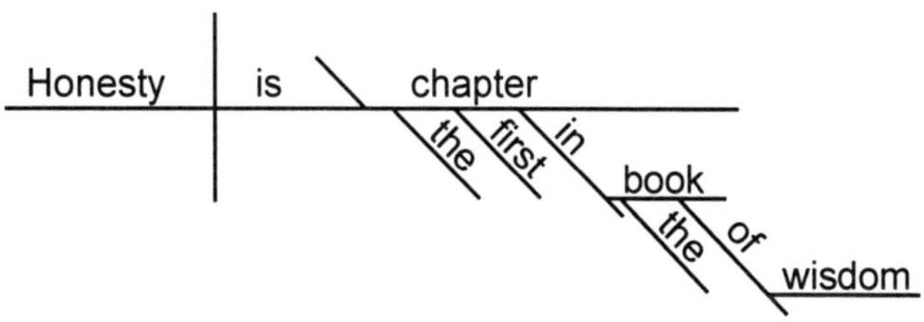

Compound Prepositional Phrases

The basis of art is truth, both in matter and in mode. –Flannery O'Connor

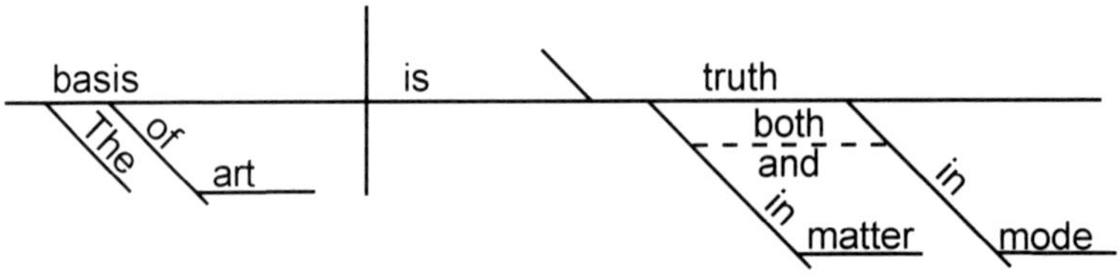

Participial Phrase

Truth, crushed to earth, shall rise again. –William Cullen Bryant

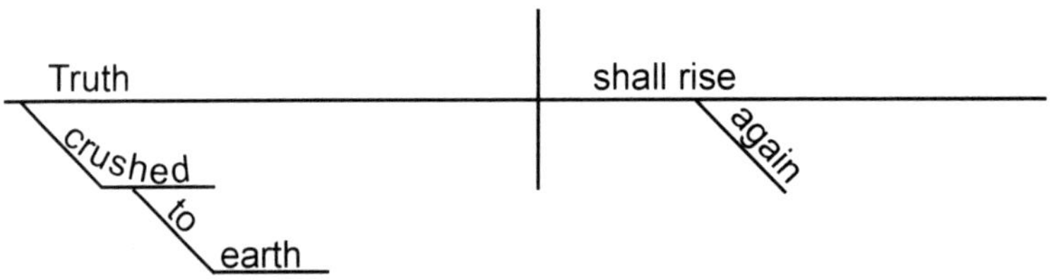

Compound Participial Phrase

Tempted by the Weird Sisters and urged on by his wife, Macbeth is thus caught between the irrational and the rational. –Cleanth Brooks

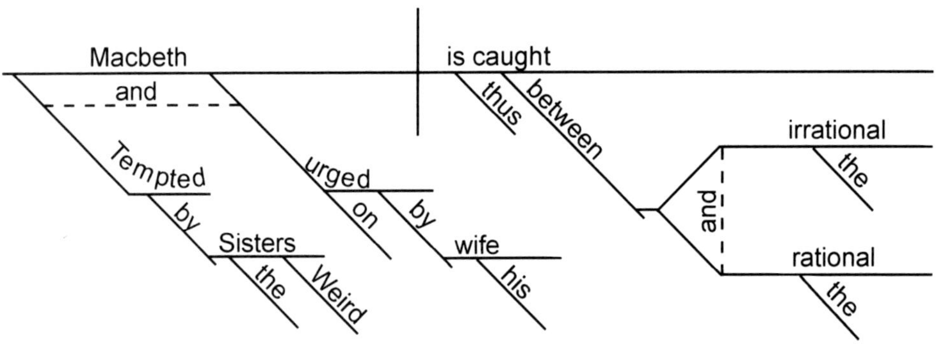

Gerund Phrase Used as a Subject

Having an intimate knowledge of your own region is not necessarily provincialism.

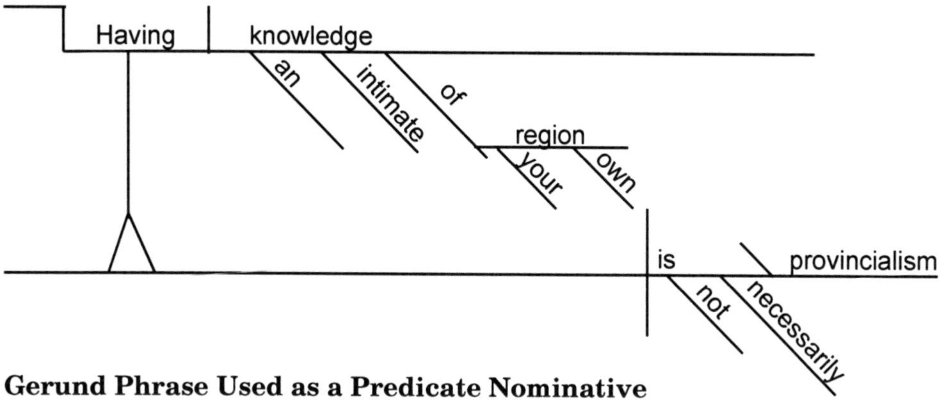

Gerund Phrase Used as a Predicate Nominative

Meditation is chewing the cud. –Thomas Watson

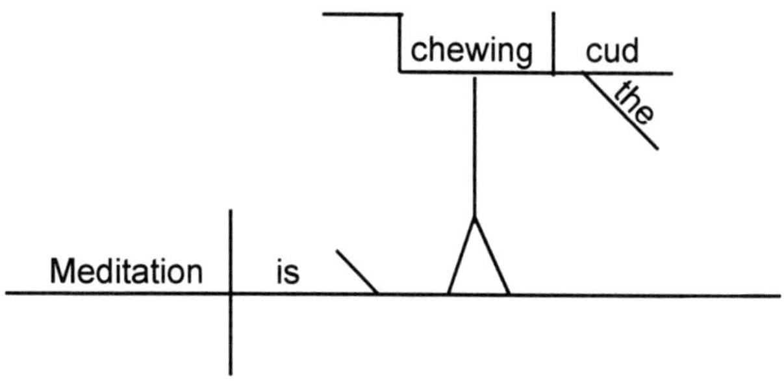

Gerund Phrase Used as a Direct Object

Have you finished reading all of Eliot's novels?

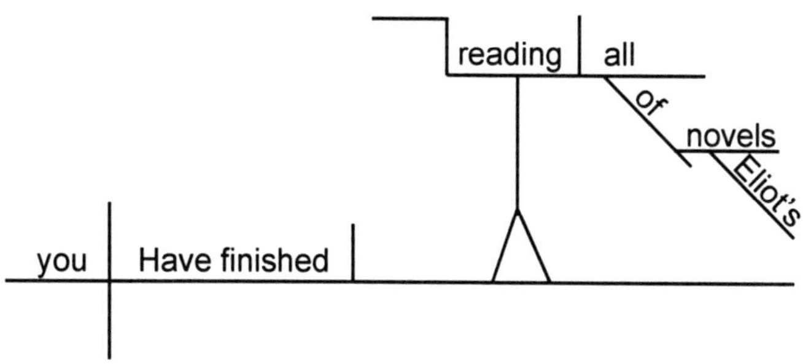

Gerund Phrase Used as an Object of a Preposition

The best means of forming a manly, virtuous, and happy people will be found in the right education of youth. –George Washington

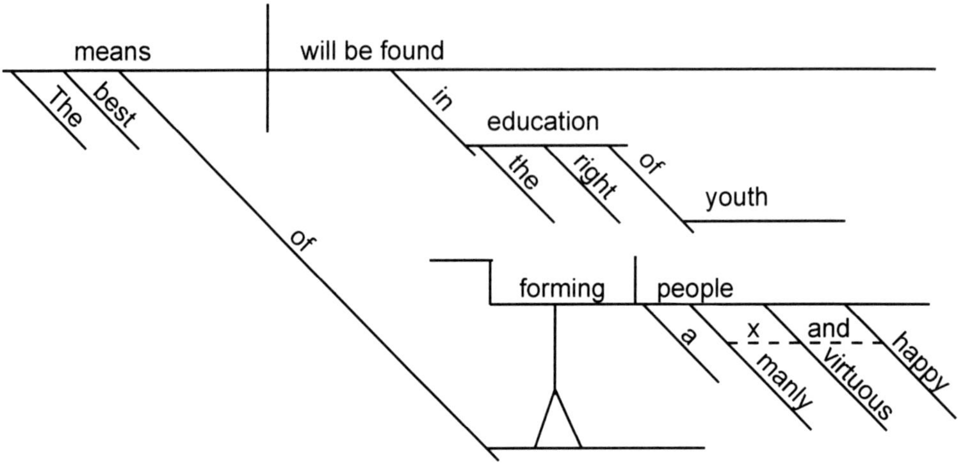

Compound Gerund Phrase

Before jumping in and starting your translation, first scan the line of poetry.

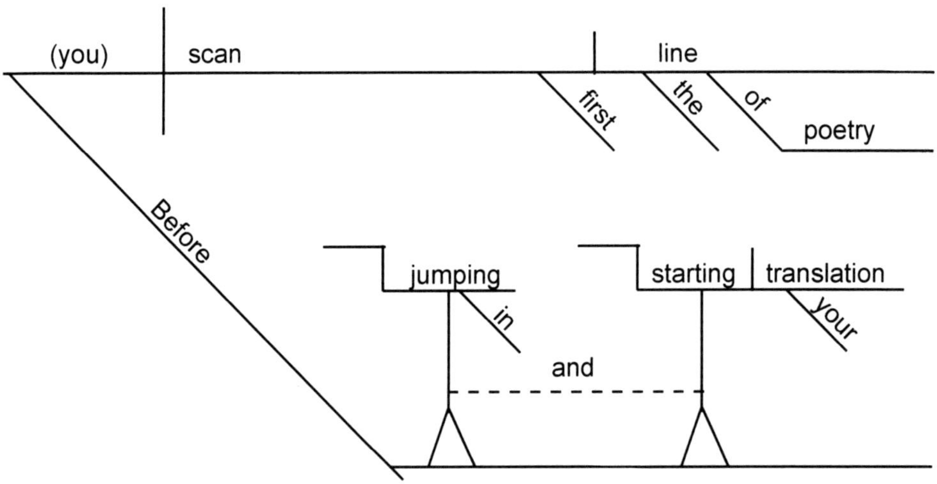

Infinitive Phrase Used as an Adjective

Which of these is the best variety to plant in this area?

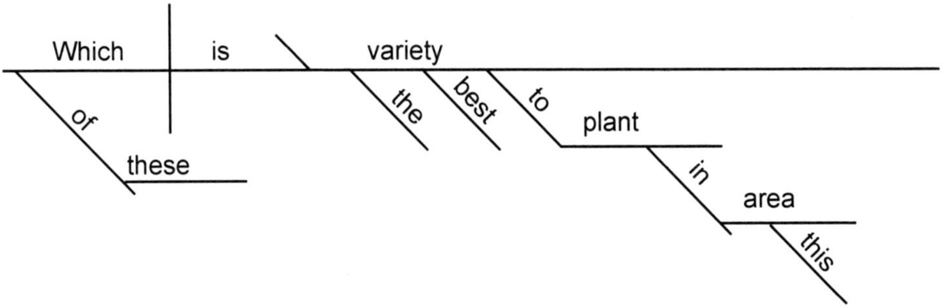

Infinitive Phrase Used as an Adverb Modifying a Verb

To make a prairie, it takes a clover and one bee. –Emily Dickinson

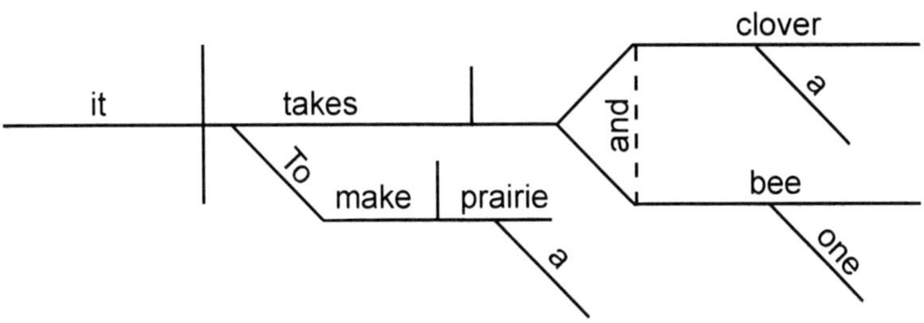

Infinitive Phrase Used as an Adverb Modifying an Adjective

I am glad to see you again.

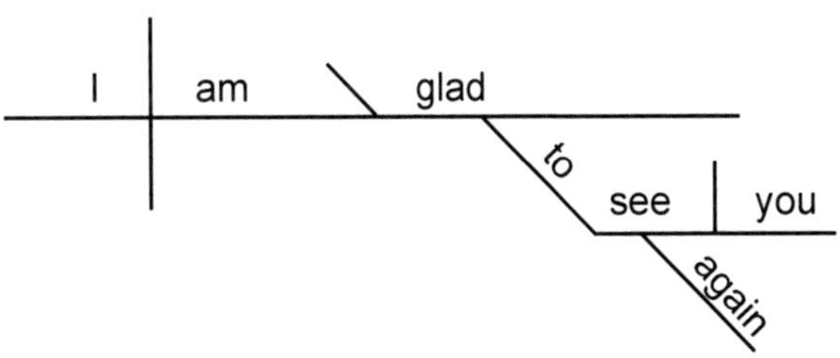

Infinitive Phrase Used as an Adverb Modifying an Adverb

Unfortunately, he did not study enough to pass the course.

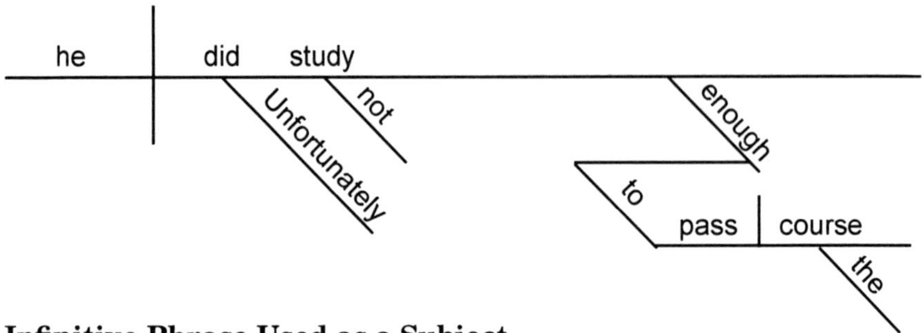

Infinitive Phrase Used as a Subject

To defend one's self, one's family, and one's possessions is the primary reason for a just war.

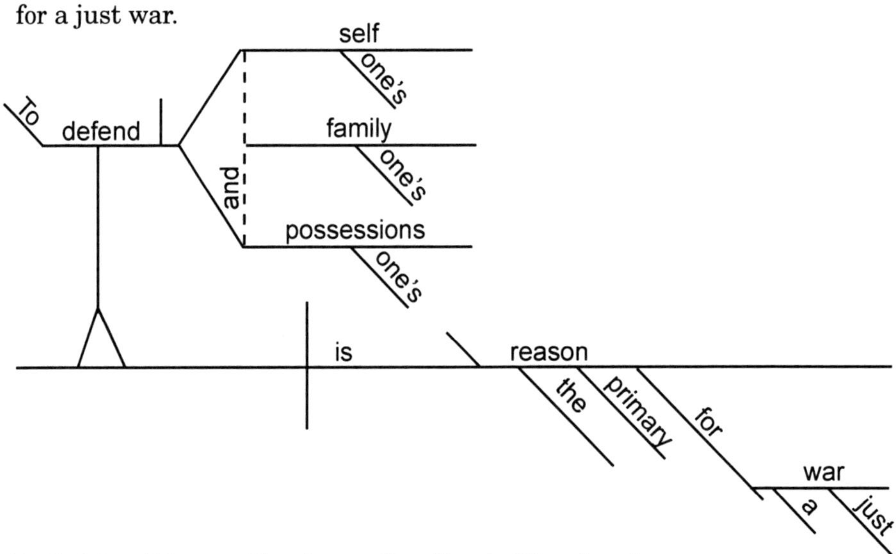

Infinitive Phrase Used as a Predicate Nominative

The true design of civil government is to protect men in the enjoyment of liberty. –Samuel West

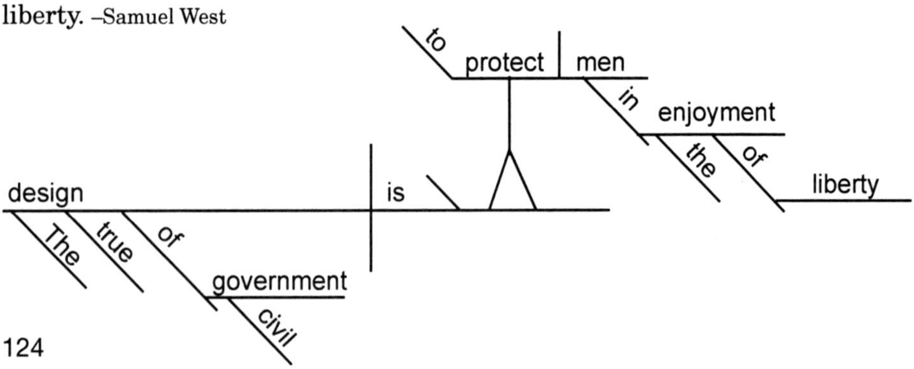

Infinitive Phrase Used as a Direct Object

I wanted merely to help them.

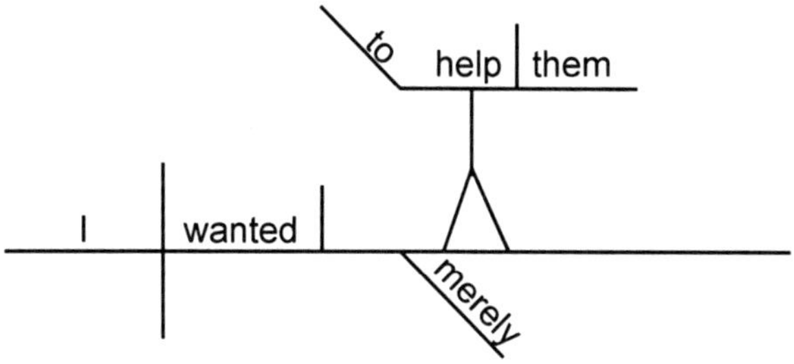

Infinitive Phrase Used as an Object of a Preposition

He did nothing but look at the pictures.

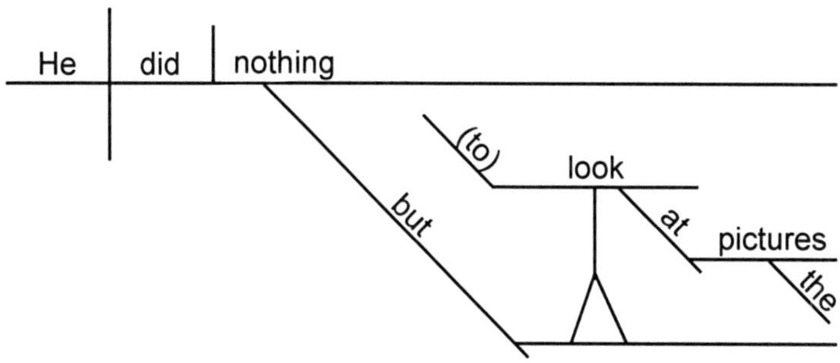

Infinitive Phrase with a Subject

The apostle wanted the Philippians to "put on the mind of Christ."

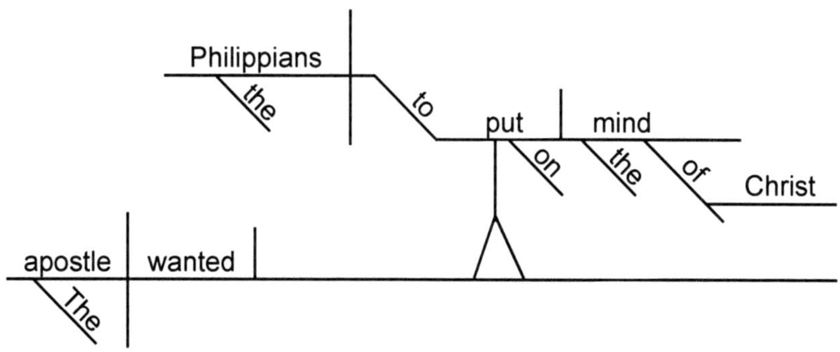

Compound Infinitive Phrase

Two of Washington's goals were to seize the Hudson and to force the British out of New York.

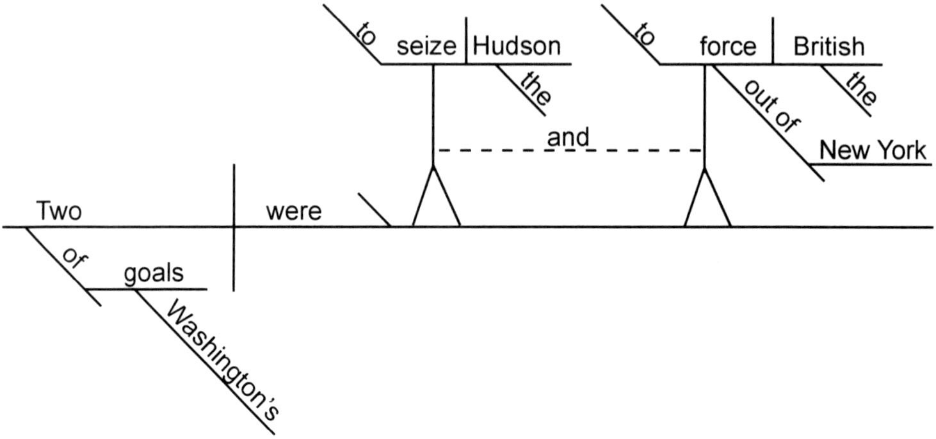

Appositive

In came Mrs. Fezziwig, one vast substantial smile. –Charles Dickens

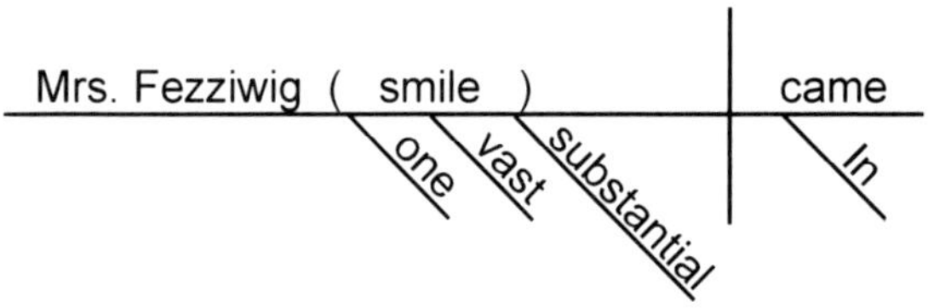

Compound Appositive

Chingachgook, Longstocking's friend and boon companion, accompanied him on his trek into the wilderness.

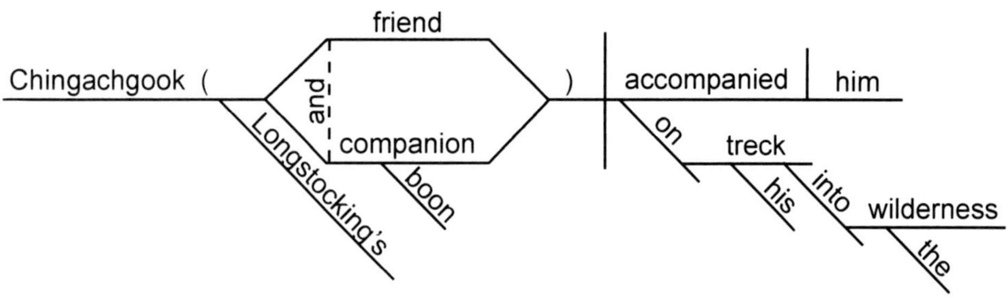

Nominative Absolute

A man in his time plays many parts, his acts being seven ages.
–William Shakespeare, *As You Like It*

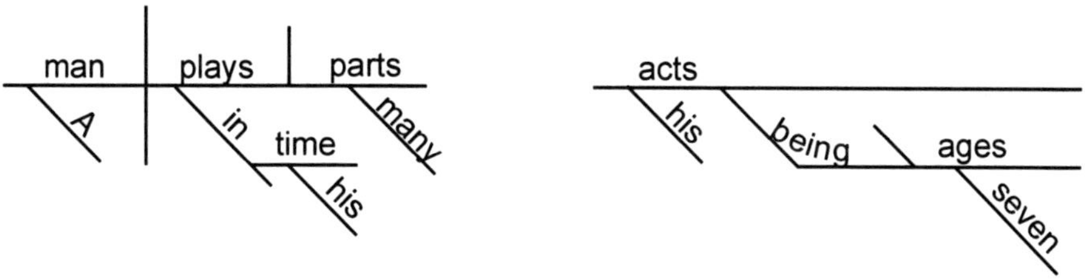

Adjective Clause

He that knows nothing will believe anything. –Thomas Fuller

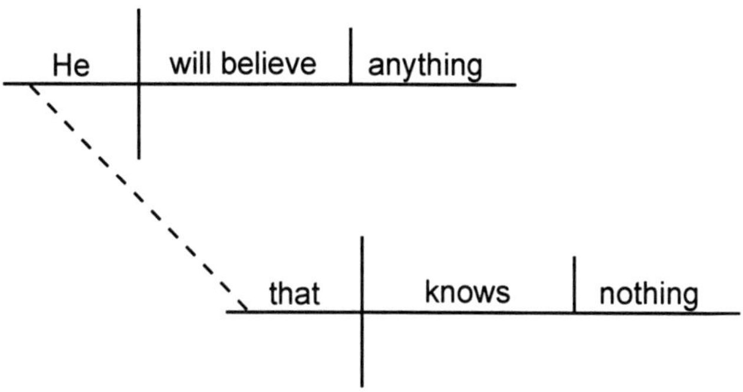

Compound Adjective Clause

They are a noble family that built this house and whose sons still live among us.

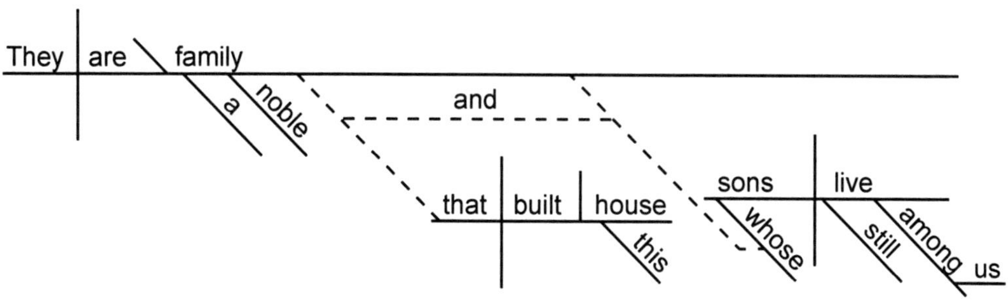

Noun Clause Used as a Subject

Who steals my purse steals trash. –William Shakespeare, *Othello*

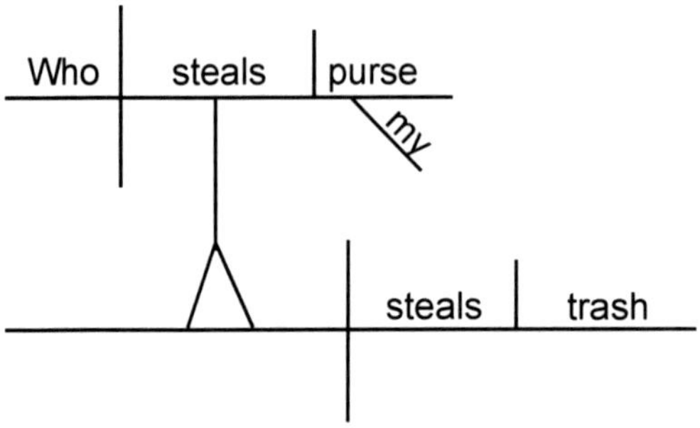

Noun Clause Used as a Predicate Nominative

Men should be what they seem. –William Shakespeare, *Othello*

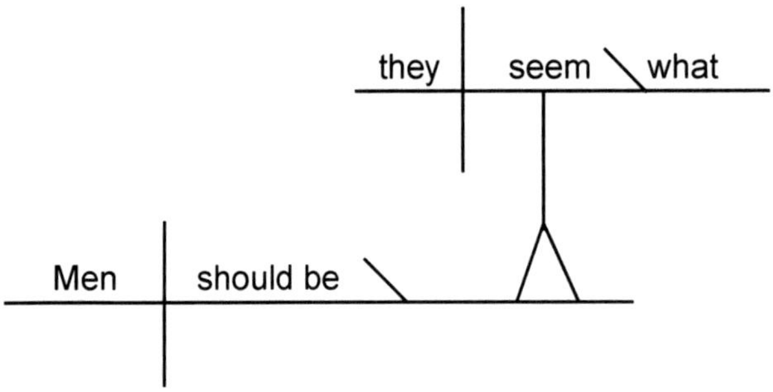

Compound Noun Clause

A bill of rights is what the people are entitled to against every government on earth, general or particular, and what no just government should refuse.
—Thomas Jefferson

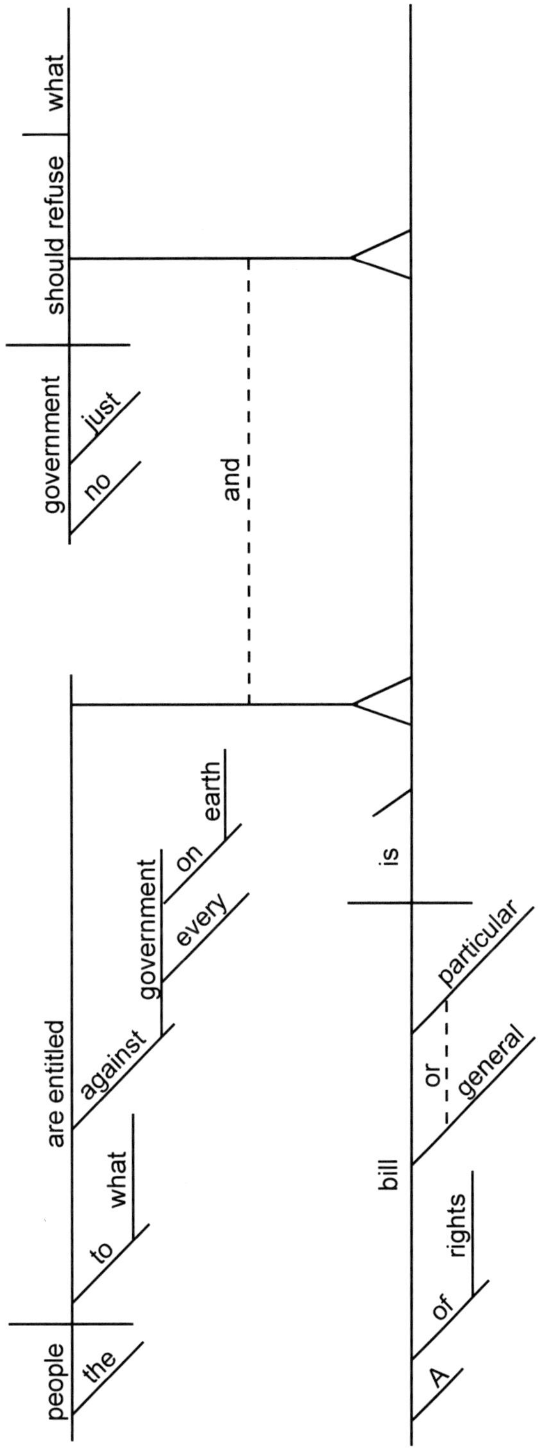

Adverb Clause Modifying a Verb

Mend your speech a little, lest you mar your fortunes.
–William Shakespeare, *King Lear*

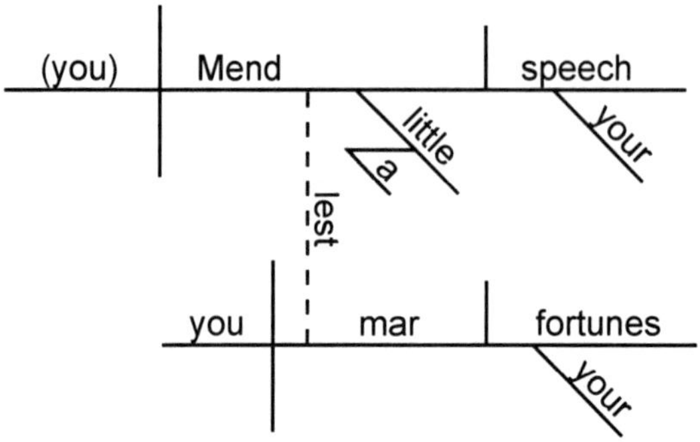

Adverb Clause Modifying an Adjective

Were you aware that this course had a prerequisite?

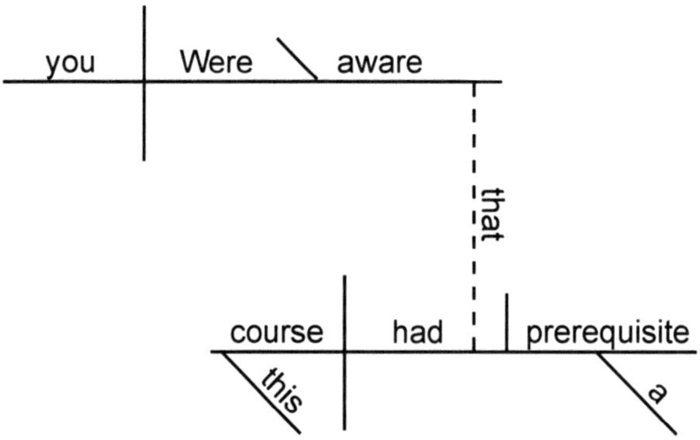

Adverb Clause Modifying an Adverb

Willoughby arrived earlier than they had expected.

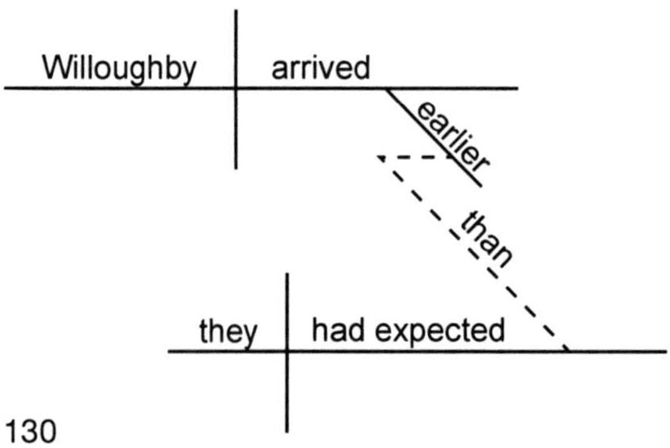

Compound Adverb Clause

Millions of spiritual creatures walk the earth unseen, both when we wake and when we sleep. –John Milton

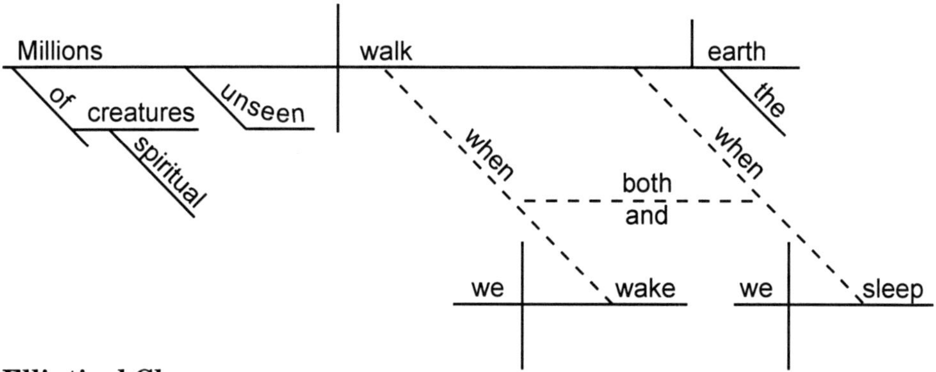

Elliptical Clause

My love's more ponderous than my tongue. –William Shakespeare, *King Lear*

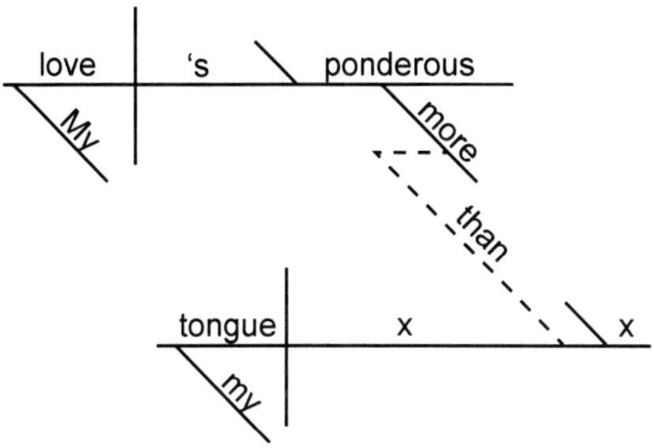

Compound Sentence

Poverty hath slain a thousand, but riches have slain ten thousand.
–Richard Greenham

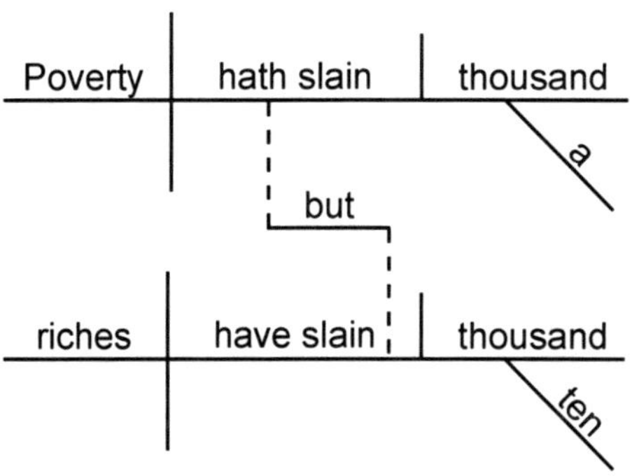

Compound-Complex Sentence

God requires satisfaction because He is holiness, but He makes satisfaction because He is love. –Augustus Strong

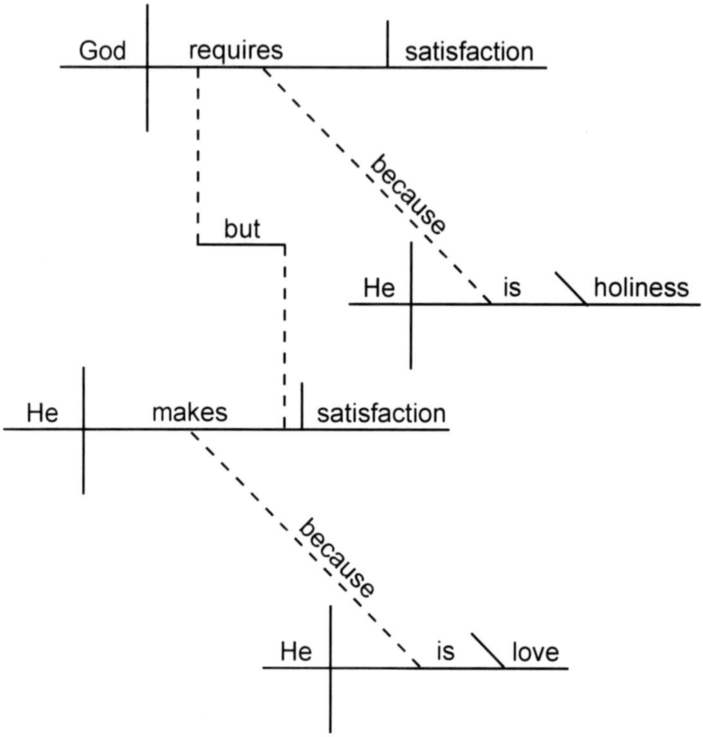

Chapter 9
Mechanics

Capitalization

Capitalize proper names and words (and abbreviations) formed from proper names.

Capitalize words referring to God.

> Trinity, Father, Son, Holy Spirit, Jehovah, Savior, Redeemer
> (The word *god* is not capitalized if it refers to heathen deities.)

Also capitalize personal pronouns referring to God.

> God created man in His own image. –Genesis 1:27

Capitalize names of individual persons (human or otherwise).

> John Taylor, Gabriel, Lucifer, Satan, the Devil, James Mason, Sr.
> (*Jr.* and *Sr.* are capitalized when following a personal name.)

Capitalize names of specific geographical areas or geographical features (such as rivers, mountains, islands, etc.).

> Europe, Great Britain, Wales, Alabama, Miller County, Appalachian Mountains, Danube River, Santa Rosa Island

Terms such as *North, South, East,* and *West* are capitalized if they are part of a recognized geographical region. However, they are not capitalized if they refer merely to direction.

> the South, the Northwest Territory, the West
> north on Highway 99, east of Montgomery

Sun and *moon* are not capitalized. *Earth* is capitalized only when it is used (without the article *the*) with other planets.

> The earth orbits around the sun.
> The nearest planets to Earth are Venus and Mars.

Capitalize names of streets, highways, bridges, monuments, and other constructions.

> Richland Avenue, Constitution Avenue, Yellowstone National Park, Golden Gate Bridge, Forty-sixth Street
> (Do not capitalize the second part of a hyphenated number used as a street name.)

Capitalize names of organizations and institutions.

> Daughters of the American Revolution, Oxford University, Folger Shakespeare Library, Department of the Treasury, Army of Northern Virginia
> (Do not capitalize the articles *a, an,* and *the* and short prepositions within a name.)

Capitalize names of historical events and periods, special events, and calendar items.

> Revolutionary War, the War Between the States, the Middle Ages, the Victorian Age, Nashville Festival of Books, Tuesday, July, Independence Day

The names of seasons (spring, summer, autumn, fall, winter) are not capitalized unless they are treated as persons.

> We have had a warmer winter this year.
> See, Winter comes to rule the varied year. –James Thomson

Capitalize names of people groups and languages.

> Japanese, Celts, Hittites, Hebrew, Cherokee

Capitalize names of religious writings and religious bodies.

> the Bible, the Pentateuch, the Beatitudes, the Dead Sea Scrolls, Judaism, Roman Catholic, Southern Methodist, Free Will Baptist,

Orthodox Presbyterian, Koran, Islam, Muslim, the Nicene Creed, the Westminster Confession

Capitalize brand names.

Dodge truck, Michelin tires, Sunbeam bread
(The common noun after the brand name is not capitalized.)

Capitalize names of particular buildings, documents, ships, courses, etc.

the White House, the Capitol, the Declaration of Independence, the Magna Charta, the *Bonhomme Richard*, the *Spirit of St. Louis,* Biology 211

Capitalize abbreviations of proper names.

FTC (Federal Trade Commission), NATO (North Atlantic Treaty Organization), UK (United Kingdom), FL (Florida), MD (Maryland), Isa. (Isaiah), 1 Cor. (1 Corinthians)
(Generally, avoid the use of abbreviations in formal writing, except for the names of well-known organizations which commonly go by their abbreviations.)

Capitalize proper adjectives and other words formed from proper names.

Scandinavian, Hispanic, Jeffersonian, Elizabethan, Shakespearean, Southern, Jewish, Biblical, Platonic, Marxism

If, through frequent use, a term derived from a proper name has lost its connection with that person, place, or thing, do not capitalize it.

pasteurize, quixotic, frankfurter, hamburger, italicize, godly

Sometimes, words develop two different uses, one capitalized and another not.

Democratic (pertaining to the Democratic Party)
democratic (pertaining to democracy)

Capitalize titles of persons.

Capitalize titles when they are used before a person's name.

> President Madison, Senator Calhoun, Queen Elizabeth II, Dr. Jerkins, Uncle Rob, Archbishop Cranmer

Do not capitalize titles when used after (or, usually, in place of) a person's name.

> James Madison, the president of the United States; John C. Calhoun, senator from South Carolina; the queen of England; my doctor; his uncle; the archbishop of Canterbury; etc.

Capitalize titles when they are used alone either in direct address or in place of the name (without the articles *a, an,* and *the*).

> Yes, Senator, here is your chair.
> Unfortunately, Mother will be in the hospital for several weeks.
> Have you bought a gift for Dad?
>
> My father was quite old when I was born.
> We visited our cousins in South Carolina.

Capitalize titles of literary works and other artistic works.

> *The Lord of the Rings* (book)
> "Bells for John Whiteside's Daughter" (poem)
> *As You Like It* (play)
> "The Displaced Person" (short story)
> "A Mighty Fortress Is Our God" (hymn)
> *The Descent from the Cross* (painting)
> *Daniel Boone Escorting Settlers Through the Cumberland Gap* (painting)
> (Do not capitalize articles, short prepositions, or conjunctions in titles unless they are the first or last words.)
>
> (Do not capitalize the article *the* when it is used before a newspaper or magazine title in a sentence.)
> the *Nashville Tennessean* (newspaper)
> the *American Organist* (magazine)

Capitalize the first word of a sentence (even one that is being quoted).

> Our goats climbed over the fence.

> As president of Washington College, Lee once said, "We have but one rule here, and it is that every student must be a gentleman."

Capitalize the personal pronoun *I* and the interjection *O*.

> Preserve me, O God: for in Thee do I put my trust. –Psalm 16:1

> (Do not capitalize the interjection *oh* unless it is the first word in a sentence.)

> Send us all the troops possible; oh, help us if you can.

Capitalize the first word in each line of a poem, even if that word does not begin a new sentence. (Some modern poets do not follow traditional capitalization or poetic usage; when quoting them, reproduce their original format.)

> And now, once more, I see young faces turn
> Where the battle is and a lonelier kildee's cry,
> Exultant with your verses to unlearn
> The bondage of their dead times' sophistry. –Donald Davidson

Punctuation

End Marks

Use appropriate end marks to indicate the end of a sentence or an abbreviation.

Use a period after a sentence making a statement or giving a command or request.

> The sky is overcast today.
> Pass the salt please.
> Close the door behind you.

Use a period after most abbreviations.

> Mr. Mrs. Dr. B.A. M.A. Ph.D. M.D.

> (Certain abbreviations [such as *AD, BC, AM, PM*] are used so commonly that periods are often omitted.)

If an organization has come to be known by its abbreviation, the periods may be omitted.

> CIA FBI NATO UN CNN ABC OPEC

Never use two periods next to each other. If an abbreviation ending in a period ends the sentence, do not use an additional period. A question mark or exclamation point may be used after a period ending an abbreviation.

> The commencement speech was given by David Johnson, Ph.D.
> Have you ever read Eudora Welty's short story "Why I Live at the P.O."?

Use a question mark after a sentence asking a question.

> What is the theme of Miller's *Death of a Salesman*?

Use an exclamation point after a sentence making an exclamation or forceful command. (Exclamation points should not be overused.)

> The stable is on fire!
> Get the horses out!

Comma

Use a comma with a coordinating conjunction (*and, but, or, nor, for, yet, so*) to join together two independent clauses into a compound sentence.

> Shakespeare lived most of his adult life in London, but he retired to Stratford, his home town.

Use commas to separate items in a series.

> Some of the "metaphysical poets" are Donne, Herbert, and Crashaw. (Notice that, in such a series, a comma is included before the conjunction between the last two items to avoid misreading. This is sometimes called the "Oxford comma.")

If there are only two items in the series, a comma is not needed.

> The fiddler played several old ballads and folk songs.

If all the items in the series are joined by conjunctions, do not use commas.

> Pecans and walnuts and almonds are high in natural fats.

Adjectives may be used in a series as well.

> From the distance we could see the vast, slow-moving tide of lava.

If an adjective and a noun are very closely related, they may be thought of as one expression. Do not treat such an adjective as part of a series of adjectives.

> The kind old man offered her his seat on the bus.

Use a comma if needed to avoid misreading.

> On the day before the rain had poured down. (unclear)
> On the day before, the rain had poured down. (clear)

Use commas to set off nonessential phrases or clauses. If a phrase or clause can be omitted without affecting the intended meaning of the sentence, it is nonessential.

> The crew who were on duty at the time of the oil spill have been questioned by authorities. (an essential adjective clause–no commas)
> Captain Hazelwood, who was on duty at the time of the oil spill, has been questioned by authorities. (a nonessential adjective clause–set off by commas)
> Who is the boy on the front row? (an essential prepositional phrase–no commas)
> Charles and Brett, in the back yard, could not hear the telephone. (a nonessential prepositional phrase–set off by commas)
> My brother Samuel studied accounting in college. (an essential appositive–no commas)
> My brother, a merchant banker in Savannah, studied accounting in college. (a nonessential appositive–set off by commas)
> The package wrapped in green paper is for you, Matt. (an essential participial phrase–no commas)
> The pioneers, looking at the distant mountains, wondered if they should ever have started their journey. (a nonessential participial phrase–set off by commas)
> You cannot enter unless you have a ticket. (an essential adverb clause–no commas)

> I went ahead and bought the binoculars, even if they were a little too expensive. (a nonessential adverb clause–set off by commas)

Use commas to set off parenthetical expressions.

> My family, by the way, migrated into Alabama from the Carolinas in 1818.

Use commas to set off interjections (such as *yes, no, well,* etc.) and words used in direct address.

> Yes, you may go with me, Son.

You may use a comma after certain introductory phrases or clauses.

> Because of his chest pain, he was taken to the hospital.
> Although we were hot and tired, we decided to go on.
> The sun having set, they made camp for the night.

But do not use commas to separate closely related items, such as subjects and verbs, verbs and complements, or modifiers and the words they are modifying.

> Learning Biblical Greek is necessary for a thorough knowledge of the New Testament.
> In our garden are roses, irises, and lavender.
> What we should do about rising inflation was the main topic of discussion.

Use a comma immediately before a quotation.

> My pastor says, "An uninformed conscience is not a reliable guide."

Use commas to separate parts of dates and addresses when they are used in a sentence. There is no comma between the month and the day or between the state and the ZIP code.

> His apartment is located at 207 Watts Circle, Nashville, Tennessee 37209.
> I began working here August 17, 1994.

Use commas after salutations in friendly letters and after the closing of both friendly and business letters.

> Dear Rob, Sincerely, Yours truly,

Semicolon

Use a semicolon to join two independent clauses into a compound sentence if there is no comma and coordinating conjunction.

> Be content with your lot; one cannot be first in everything. –Aesop

If there are commas within the clauses, you may use a semicolon with the coordinating conjunction in place of yet another comma.

> The question was put to Aristotle, what hope is; and his answer was, "It is the dream of a waking man." –Diogenes Laertius

Transitional words (such as *accordingly, consequently, for example, for instance, however, namely, nevertheless, that is, thus*) after a semicolon are usually followed by a comma.

> The wise steward, to whom five talents had been given, had used his talents wisely; consequently, he obtained five more.

Use semicolons between items in a series if there are commas within the items.

> We visited several historic homes in Virginia: Mount Vernon, the home of George Washington; Monticello, the home of Thomas Jefferson; and Montpelier, the home of James Madison.

Colon

Whereas a comma is usually used before a quotation, use a colon before a quotation that is introduced formally.

> Let me quote the immortal Bard: "O it is excellent to have a giant's strength, but it is tyrannous to use it like a giant."
> Isabella replied to Lucio, "O it is excellent to have a giant's strength, but it is tyrannous to use it like a giant."

Colons and dashes are exactly opposite. A colon is used before a list or other material that explains what comes before the colon. A dash is used after a list or other material that explains what comes after the dash.

Use a colon before a list, especially after such expressions as *the following* or *as follows*. (If the list is used as a complement or the object of a preposition, do not use a colon before it.)

> Our itinerary will be as follows: London on Monday, Oxford on Tuesday, and Stonehenge on Wednesday.
> We visited London on Monday, Oxford on Tuesday, and Stonehenge on Wednesday.

Use a colon instead of a semicolon between two independent clauses if the second one explains the first one.

> The exercises prescribed by his physician produced the desired result: the muscles of his legs were significantly strengthened.

Use a colon between the chapter and verse of a Bible reference and between the hour and minute and between the minute and second of a time reference.

> Genesis 3:15 Isaiah 9:6-7 4:17 PM

Use colons after salutations of business letters.

> Dear sir or madam: Dear Senator Hawkins:

Dash

As stated above, in many ways a dash is actually the opposite of a colon. Whereas a colon comes before the list or other material that explains what comes before the colon, a dash comes after the list or other material that explains what will come after the dash.

> John Jay, Alexander Hamilton, and James Madison–these were the writers responsible for *The Federalist Papers*.

Though dashes are often used in informal writing to indicate sentence breaks, generally do not do this in formal composition.

Parentheses

Use parentheses to set off brief explanatory information, especially if that information is grammatically unconnected with the rest of the sentence.

Zimbabwe (formerly Rhodesia) has lurched from one political tragedy to another.
The paramecium is usually oval-shaped (see figure 18).
Margaret Thatcher (now Lady Thatcher) spoke eloquently at President Reagan's funeral.

Brackets

Use brackets to indicate any additions, corrections, or changes in a quotation.

Benjamin Hill said, "He [General Lee] was a foe without hate, a friend without treachery, a soldier without cruelty, and a victim without murmuring."
The speaker concluded with these words: "On that day [September 11, 2001], the United States of America turned a fateful corner in her political life."

Quotation Marks

Use quotation marks to set off a direct quotation.

The Book of Common Prayer gives this definition of sin: "We have left undone those things which we ought to have done, and we have done those things which we ought not to have done."

Do not use quotation marks to set off an indirect quotation.

Our teacher said that we had three minutes left in the examination period.

Remember to capitalize the first word of a quoted sentence, whether it comes at the beginning of the quotation or later. Do not capitalize the first word of a quotation if it is not a complete sentence.

"Of making many books," said the Preacher, "there is no end."
"I would rather be attacked than unnoticed," said Samuel Johnson. "The worst thing you can do to an author is to be silent as to his works."
We, like the patriarchs of old, "desire a better country, that is, an heavenly."

Periods and commas go inside closing quotation marks. Semicolons and colons go outside closing quotation marks. Question marks and exclamation points go inside if they pertain to the quoted matter, but outside if they pertain to the entire sentence.

> Richard Baxter said that he preached "as a dying man to dying men."
> "Neither a borrower, nor a lender be," says Polonius to Laertes.
> Caesar said to the soothsayer, "The ides of March have come"; the soothsayer replied, "Yes, but they are not past."
> "Look at what you have done!" cried his mother.
> Who described Washington as "first in war, first in peace, and first in the hearts of his countrymen"?
> He heard a voice saying, "Saul, Saul, why persecutest thou me?"

If you are quoting more than one sentence, put quotation marks only at the beginning and at the end of the entire quotation.

> Our Lord said to His disciples, "Ye are the light of the world. A city that is set on an hill cannot be hid."

If you are quoting more than one paragraph, put quotation marks at the beginning of each paragraph and at the end of the last quoted paragraph.

(Usually, in college compositions, a quotation that would take more than seven lines of type should be set off, without quotation marks, in a block quotation.)

Whereas italics (described later) are used for titles of books or magazines, use quotation marks for parts of books or magazines, such as names of short stories, short poems, songs, chapters, essays, and articles.

> The opening chapter of Dickens's autobiographical novel is entitled "I Am Born."
> The congregation rose and sang the old hymn "Abide with Me."
> In the speech contest, Christine recited the haunting poem "The Highwayman."
> The choir sang the majestic "Hallelujah Chorus" from Handel's *Messiah*.

If something within a quotation needs quotation marks, use single quotation marks.

> "Who wrote 'Stopping by Woods on a Snowy Evening'?" asked Miss Pugh.

Italics

Italics is a special type font developed in Italy early in the sixteenth century. It is used in printed type (including material printed on a word processor) to indicate some special usage. In handwriting, these special uses are indicated by underlining.

Use italics for the title of books, magazines, plays, paintings, sculptures, other works of art, and the names of newspapers, ships, trains, aircraft, and spacecraft.

David Copperfield (book)
National Geographic (magazine)
Measure for Measure (play)
The Night Watch (painting)
The Discus Thrower (sculpture)
Bonhomme Richard (ship)
The Spirit of St. Louis (airplane)
Challenger (spacecraft)

The articles *a, an,* and *the* before a title or name are italicized only if they are part of the actual title or name. The article *the* before the name of a magazine or newspaper is not usually italicized.

the *Atlantic Monthly* the *Wall Street Journal*

Use italics for foreign words or expressions that have not been accepted into the English language.

mutatis mutandis *in flagrante delicto*

However, do not use italics for foreign words or expressions that have become part of the English language.

non sequitur ipso facto hoi polloi

Use italics for words, letters, and numbers which are being referred to as such within the sentence.

The words *proceed* and *precede* are often misspelled.
Do not use &'s in formal composition.

Hyphen

Use a hyphen to divide a word at the end of a line. (See the discussion of word division below.)

Use a hyphen for compound numbers from twenty-one through ninety-nine.

twenty-three inches	fifty-eight names

Use a hyphen in compound adjectives.

a two-story house	a three-year-old child
a bright-colored blouse	cream-filled doughnuts

Use a hyphen in fractions used as adjectives.

This recipe requires a two-thirds cup of milk.
Two thirds of the clay tiles were broken.

Use a hyphen with all prefixes before proper names and with the prefixes *all-*, *ex-*, *self-*, and the suffix *-elect*.

anti-Semitic	neo-Platonic	un-Biblical	non-Christian
all-inclusive	ex-governor	self-interest	president-elect

Apostrophe

Use an apostrophe to form the possessive case of nouns and indefinite pronouns.

Form the possessive case of a singular noun by adding an apostrophe and an *s*.

the boy's cap	his boss's orders
Dickens's novels	Mr. Schwartz's market

However, form the possessive case of the following by adding only an apostrophe: ancient proper names ending in *-es*, *Jesus*, and expressions such as *for goodness' sake*.

Sophocles' play	for conscience' sake
Jesus' baptism	Moses' brother

Form the possessive case of a plural noun not ending in *s* by adding an apostrophe and an *s*.

the children's games	the oxen's yoke
men's clothing	the sheep's fleeces

Form the possessive case of a plural noun ending in *s* by adding only an apostrophe.

the boys' caps	the Smiths' house
the horses' stalls	books' covers

Form the possessive case of a compound word or words showing joint possession by making the last word possessive.

father-in-law's birthplace	Dan and Alice's children
board of trustees' meeting	Herriot and Haskell's Grocery Store

(If the two words showing joint possession include a possessive pronoun as the second word, make the first word possessive.)

Bob's and my apartment

(If several nouns indicate individual possession rather than joint possession, make each of the nouns possessive.)

Dr. Berger's and Dr. Keiler's patients

Form the possessive case of an indefinite pronoun by adding an apostrophe and an *s*. Do not use apostrophes for personal pronouns in the possessive case or for the pronoun *whose*.

somebody's notebook	his homework
everyone's assistance	its burrow
whose house	next to theirs

Use an apostrophe in a contraction to show that a letter has been omitted. (Remember however, that contractions are not used in formal composition.)

can't	shouldn't	weren't

Use an apostrophe and an *s* to form the plurals of letters, numbers, signs, and words referred to as words.

cross your *t*'s	all of your *7*'s
leave out the *and*'s	the *q*'s

Never use an apostrophe to form the plural of a noun.

> They have fresh egg's for sale. (incorrect)
> They have fresh eggs for sale. (correct)

An apostrophe is not needed to form the plural of a year written in numerals.

> 1990s

Slash

Use a slash to indicate line divisions when quoting poetry within a sentence.

> Robert Herrick reminds his readers: "Gather ye rosebuds while ye may, / Old Time is still a-flying."

Ellipsis Marks

Use ellipsis marks (three periods with no spaces between them but a space before and after them) to indicate the omission of something from a quotation.

> The author of the Epistle to the Hebrews says of Abraham, "He looked for a city ... whose builder and maker is God."

Do not begin a quotation with ellipsis marks.

> "... He does not press men," says Donne in one of his sermons; "Christ is served with voluntaries." (incorrect)
> "He does not press men," says Donne in one of his sermons; "Christ is served with voluntaries." (correct)

If ellipsis marks are needed at the end of a sentence, first put a period at the end of the sentence, then a space before the first ellipsis mark.

> Donne says of death: "Be not proud, though some have called thee / Mighty and dreadful, for thou art not so. ..."

When omitting an entire line from a quoted poem, use periods with spaces between them for the approximate length of the omitted line.

> So through the Plymouth woods John Alden went on his errand;
> . . . .

Saw the new-built house, and people at work in a meadow;
Heard, as he drew near the door, the musical voice of Priscilla
Singing the hundredth Psalm, the grand old Puritan anthem,

. . . .

Then, as he opened the door, he beheld the form of the maiden
Seated beside her wheel, and the carded wool like a snow-drift
Piled at her knee, her white hands feeding the ravenous spindle,
While with her foot on the treadle she guided the wheel in its motion.

Manuscript Form

Abbreviations

Abbreviations are commonly used before or after names. Some abbreviated titles precede names (such as *Mr., Mrs., Dr.*, etc.). In scholarly writing, abbreviations of academic degrees frequently follow names: *B.A., B.S., M.A., M.Div., Ph.D., M.D., J.D.*, etc. When following a name these academic degrees are preceded by a comma. Also, do not use both a title and an academic degree with the same name.

Kevin Hester, M.Div. (correct)
Kevin Hester, Ph.D. (correct)
Dr. Kevin Hester, Ph.D. (incorrect)

The abbreviations *Jr.* and *Sr.*, which follow personal names, are preceded by a comma. However, similar descriptions written as Roman numerals are not.

Matthew Pinson, Jr.	Henry VIII
David Bergsen, Sr.	Gerald W. Harrison III

The expressions *Reverend* and *Honorable* (frequently abbreviated as *Rev.* and *Hon.*) are not really titles at all, but honorific adjectives. They are used only before a full name or a name with an appropriate title. They are not used independently as names. If preceded by the word *the*, then they are not abbreviated, but written out.

Rev. Quincy (incorrect)
Rev. James Quincy (correct)
Rev. Dr. Quincy (correct)
the Rev. James Quincy (incorrect)
the Reverend James Quincy (correct)

> Hon. Gustafson (incorrect)
> Hon. Neil Gustafson (correct)
> Hon. Mr. Gustafson (correct)
> the Hon. Neil Gustafson (incorrect)
> the Honorable Neil Gustafson (correct)

The time designations *AM* (*ante meridiem*, meaning "before noon") and *PM* (*post meridiem*, meaning "after noon") may be used with or without periods, either capitalized or not. Given their meanings, they should not be combined with such expressions as "in the morning" or "in the afternoon." Similarly, *o'clock* ("of the clock") should not be used with *AM* or *PM* or with numerals.

> The meeting starts at 7:00 PM in the evening. (incorrect)
> The meeting starts at 7:00 PM o'clock. (incorrect)
> The meeting starts at 7:00 in the evening. (correct)
> The meeting starts at 7:00 PM. (correct)
> The meeting starts at seven o'clock in the evening. (correct)

The date designations *AD* (*Anno Domini*, meaning "in the year of the Lord") and *BC* (*Before Christ*) indicate the number of years of an event before or after the birth of Jesus Christ. They may be used with or without periods, but they are always capitalized. Note also that *AD* is written before a date but *BC* after a date. A date without a designation is presumed to be *AD*.

> The city of Rome was founded in 753 BC.
> The death of the last Roman emperor in AD 476 spelled the end of the Roman Empire.
> Charlemagne, who established his empire in 800, attempted to revive use of the title "Emperor of the Romans."

Become familiar with abbreviations that are frequently used in scholarly writing: *c.* or *ca.* (*circa*, meaning "around"); *cf.* (*confer*, meaning "compare"); *e.g.* (*exempli gratia*, meaning "for the sake of an example" or "for example"); *et al.* (*et alii*, meaning "and others"); and *i.e.*, (*id est*, meaning "that is"). Such expressions may or may not be italicized.

> Kings of the Merovingian dynasty ruled the Franks for two hundred years beginning ca. 500.
> Cf. Acts 17.
> English nouns with plurals ending in *en* (e.g., *child*, *man*, *ox*) are Old English or Anglo-Saxon in origin.
> Giotto, Massaccio, et al. represent a major shift in European art.

During the reign of Queen Victoria (i.e., 1837-1901), Great Britain underwent profound changes in culture, technology, politics, and religion.
(Notice that the abbreviations *e.g.* and *i.e.* are followed by a comma. Also, the word *et* in *et al.* is not an abbreviation and is not followed by a period.)

Numbers

Generally, except in scientific contexts, if a number can be written out in one or two words, do not use numerals.

	forty	forty-seven
	two thousand	fifteen hundred
but	672	83,246

However, always use numerals for years.

483 BC AD 68

Do not mix numerals and written-out numbers of one or two words. If using both, use numerals for all of them.

Of the 120 homes to be built, fifty-eight have been completed. (incorrect)
Of the 120 homes to be built, 58 have been completed. (correct)

Do not start a sentence with numerals.

3,280 people attended last year's annual convention. (incorrect)
Last year's convention was attended by 3,280 people. (correct)
Over three thousand people attended last year's convention. (correct)

Do not use such abbreviations as *1st, 2nd, 3rd, 4th*, etc.; rather, write the expression out.

The horse which was favored actually came in 3rd place. (incorrect)
The horse which was favored actually came in third place. (correct)

Word Division

At the end of a line, you may divide a word at a syllable break with a hyphen.

Of course, one-syllable words cannot be divided.

pray-ed (incorrect)	prayed (correct)

Avoid dividing after or before a one- or two-letter syllable.

crook-ed (incorrect)	crooked (correct)
to-day (incorrect)	today (correct)
a-bout (incorrect)	about (correct)

If a word contains a prefix or suffix, use that as the place of division.

antedi-luvian (incorrect)	ante-diluvian (correct)

Words that double a consonant before a suffix should be divided between those doubled letters. (However, words that already end in double consonants before suffixes are added should not be divided between the double consonants.)

rebell-ing (incorrect)	rebel-ling (correct)
for-getting (incorrect)	forget-ting (correct)
er-ring (incorrect)	err-ing (correct)

Divide hyphenated compound words at the hyphen.

self-absorbed
ex-governor

Do not divide proper names.

Chapter 10
Diction

Using the Dictionary

For a careful writer a good dictionary is indispensable. No doubt you will use it for looking up the correct spelling and meaning of words, but you will also find that it has a wealth of other information in it as well. Become familiar with the different kinds of dictionaries and with the different sorts of information included in the dictionary.

Kinds of Dictionaries

There are specialized dictionaries dealing with all sorts of different information (geographical dictionaries, Bible dictionaries, scientific dictionaries, etc.). We are concerned here with dictionaries of English words, specifically general dictionaries. (There are other dictionaries dealing with specialized branches of English: American slang, Scots English, poetic diction, etc.) General dictionaries come, basically, in three varieties: unabridged dictionaries, college dictionaries, and pocket dictionaries.

Unabridged dictionaries contain about 500,000 words. They are called unabridged because they have not been shortened down from a longer work. These dictionaries are quite large and very expensive; therefore, generally you will find them in your college library, or perhaps in a writing laboratory. Some of the best one-volume unabridged dictionaries are these:

> *The Random House Dictionary of the English Language*, Second Edition
> *Webster's New International Dictionary of the English Language*, Second Edition
> *Webster's Third New International Dictionary of the English Language*

College (or collegiate or desk) dictionaries are abridged dictionaries and contain approximately 150,000 words. Everyone who works with words, including all college students, needs to own a good college dictionary. Some of the best college dictionaries are these:

The American Heritage Dictionary of the English Language
Merriam Webster's Collegiate Dictionary
The New Oxford American Dictionary
The Random House College Dictionary
Webster's New World Dictionary of the American Language

Pocket dictionaries are short, little dictionaries, giving brief definitions of a few hundred words at most. Though these may be useful for looking up the spelling of a word, you should not depend on them for scholarly information. They are insufficient for a college student.

Become very familiar with your college dictionary. The more familiar you are with it, the more you will use it. Although most good college dictionaries are more or less alike, the arrangement of information may be different. Where are biographical or geographical names located? Where are abbreviations located? They may be in the main body of the text, or they may be arranged in special listings at the back. Where is the etymology (the history of the word) given, before the definition or after it? One real concern to any serious user of a dictionary (whether a college student or not) is the dictionary's usage labels. Examine your dictionary to see whether it includes usage labels to help its users understand adequately the contexts in which words which are not universally accepted should be used. (If it does not give sufficient usage labels, it is probably not a good college dictionary.)

Information Found in Dictionary Entries

Much valuable information can be found in each entry in a good dictionary.

The entry word is the word or phrase which is being defined. Entry words are listed alphabetically; entries made up of more than one word or hyphenated entries are alphabetized as if there were no spaces or hyphens between the words.

Variant spellings are usually given. If two or more spellings are separated with commas or the word *or*, they may be considered equally acceptable. If the variant spelling is preceded by the word *also*, then the first spelling is preferable.

Capitalization will be indicated, either in the entry word itself or in the body of the entry with some label, such as "cap." or "usu. cap."

The pronunciation is generally printed within parentheses immediately after the entry word. Various dictionaries use different systems of indicating pronunciation. Become familiar with the pronunciation key for your dictionary. Pronunciation symbols may be located at the front of your dictionary; some dictionaries also list the most common pronunciation symbols at the foot of pages, regularly, throughout the dictionary. In addition to letters for certain sounds, most dictionaries use symbols called diacritical marks to indicate various vowel sounds. Become familiar with the most common pronunciation symbols.

Symbols for vowel sounds

The breve (˘) indicates a short vowel sound, as in *hat*.
The macron (¯) indicates a long vowel sound, as in *hate*.
The dieresis (¨) indicates a broad vowel sound, as in *bald*.
The schwa (ə) indicates an unaccented vowel with an "uh" sound, as in *about*.

Symbols for consonant sounds
Usually the consonant itself is used to indicate its sound, but a few consonants produce different sounds in different situations. These are some of the most common:

hard k sound	=	k
soft c	=	s
ph	=	f
soft g	=	j
t or s, as in *caution* or *sure*	=	sh
s, as in *used*	=	z

The respelling to indicate pronunciation will divide the word into syllables either by leaving spaces between them or by putting dashes or hyphens between them. It will indicate which syllables should be stressed by inserting accent marks. Some dictionaries indicate a primary stress with a heavy accent mark (ˊ) and a secondary stress with a lighter accent mark (ˊ). Become familiar with your dictionary so that you understand its markings for pronunciation.

The entry will also include the part of speech of the entry word. Some of the abbreviations used most commonly are

n. (noun)
pl. n. (noun used only in the plural, like *scissors*)
v. or vb. (verb)
pron. (pronoun)

adj. (adjective)
adv. (adverb)
prep. (preposition)
conj. (conjunction)
interj. (interjection)
v.t. or trans. (transitive verb)
v.i. or intr. (intransitive verb)

The entry will also give the various changes of spelling which indicate different uses. These are called inflections or inflected forms. Some of the inflected forms that may be given in your dictionary are the plural (especially if it is irregular), the principal parts of verbs, and comparative and superlative degree forms of adjectives and adverbs.

The etymology or history of a word will probably precede or follow the definition. As you may know, English has borrowed the vast majority of its vocabulary from other languages. Dictionaries will normally indicate the source of a word with an abbreviation, such as AS (Anglo-Saxon), OE (Old English), ME (Middle English), F. (French), G. (German), Gr. (Greek), L. (Latin), ON (Old Norse), Sp. (Spanish), etc. Become familiar with the location of the etymologies in your dictionary and with the abbreviations used in them.

If an entry word (or a specific definition of a particular entry word) is limited to some particular usage, your dictionary will probably include a restrictive label. These labels may indicate that it is used in some particular field of study (architecture, biology, sports, etc.). They may indicate that the word is used in certain particular geographical areas (dialect, regional, Southern U.S., British, etc.). They may indicate that the word is no longer used in common speech but is now used only in certain historical or poetic contexts (archaic, obsolete, poetic, etc.).

The most important restrictive label a dictionary can give is probably the usage label. Certain words (whether they have been in the language for a short time or a long time) have never become completely accepted. They may be considered slang, informal or colloquial, substandard or nonstandard, or even vulgar or profane. A good dictionary will label these words and indicate that they are not considered standard English. Beginning with the publication of the *Webster's Third New International Dictionary of the English Language*, published in 1961, some dictionaries have begun to limit their usage labels. For instance, many words which had been labeled "slang" in *Webster's New International Dictionary of the English Language*, Second Edition, and which were still of questionable acceptance were nonetheless without label in the Third Edition. Though the Third Edition does give many usage notes and example sentences (many of which were designed to describe the proper contexts in which certain unlabeled words should be used), its limited use of usage labels has unfortunately tended to encourage other unabridged and college dictionaries to limit them as well. Examine your dictionary to see whether it gives usage labels to help its users adequately understand the limited contexts in which words that are not universally accepted should be used. In certain situations, a dictionary may give a usage note rather than merely a one-word label. Such notes are extremely valuable to the person who wants to speak and write properly.

Every language has expressions or phrases which make sense only in that language and cannot be translated literally; such expressions are called idioms. Dictionaries normally give these under the key word in the expression. For instance, "a feather in one's cap" may be located under *feather*.

Additionally, dictionaries may give synonyms, antonyms, illustrations, charts, scientific information (such as scientific names of plants and animals), and encyclopedic information (biographical or geographical names or historical information). Check your dictionary to see what kinds of information can be found in it.

Using Appropriate Language

A good speaker or writer knows the audience he is addressing and the context in which he is working. He will therefore want his speech or writing to be appropriate to the situation. There are three levels of English usage: standard formal, standard informal, and substandard.

Standard formal English is the type of language you should adopt in all formal situations, in research papers and other collegiate compositions, and in formal letter-writing. Of course, it uses only correct grammar. But it also avoids such things as contractions and informal language (including slang).

Standard informal (or colloquial) English is the language used in everyday conversation. It will include contractions and may include language which is not completely acceptable in the most formal settings.

Substandard English is incorrect English and is the language of the uneducated. Such language is filled with errors in usage, especially in the usage of verbs, pronouns, adjectives, and adverbs. As a college student, you should avoid this type of language both in formal and informal situations.

Traditionally, in the days before popular media (radio, movies, and television, especially), various geographical regions of any language group developed their own dialects or language varieties. This was as true of English as of other languages. In the British Isles, in addition to such non-English languages as Welsh, Scots Gaelic, and Irish Gaelic, there developed regional dialects or varieties. Many of these were transported to the English colonies in America and elsewhere. As a result of the various places in Britain where its original English-speaking settlers came from, America developed several regional dialects. The four oldest regional forms of American English were those in New England, in the Middle Colonies (such as Pennsylvania), in the Deep South, and in the Appalachian South. Later other varieties developed, especially in the West and among the descendants of African slaves. Each variety or dialect of American English brought with it special pronunciations and even its own vocabulary.

Unfortunately, the popular media have had a homogenizing effect on American English (as well as on English in other countries). Some have mistakenly considered one variety of English superior to another. It is important to distinguish between levels of usage (standard formal, standard informal, and substandard) described above and regional or ethnic varieties. If you are fortunate enough to have a regional or ethnic accent, do not try to get rid of it or to adopt the homogenized, non-dialect of television. In a world that is becoming increasing globalized and is frequently disparaging of regional local cultures, our language varieties or dialects help keep us connected with our families and our past. In a country like the United States, our various dialects and language varieties can add verve and vitality to our literary life. As an educated speaker of English, you can still maintain the regional or ethnic pronunciation, vocabulary, and idiom of your heritage, while speaking and writing correct English.

Unlike dialectal varieties which developed organically over long periods of time, slang is a product of popular culture. Though it may be colorful or vivid, it is also usually quite transitory and sometimes even crude. Slang rapidly becomes dated and passé. You will certainly want to avoid it in formal speaking and writing.

Slang may have its uses in certain limited contexts, but there are two types of language which should never be part of your language: vulgarity and profanity. Vulgar language (from the Latin word *vulgus*, meaning "the illiterate masses") frequently includes language which is indecent, coarse, or even obscene. A word which an uneducated person might use naively or unknowingly cannot be used by an educated person except for shock value. Such language should not be part of your speech or writing. Use your language effectively, powerfully, even fiercely if necessary, but do not use it merely to shock or to embarrass others. Vulgarity marks a person as uncultured or, even worse, uncaring and uncharitable. The word *profanity* comes from two Latin words meaning "outside the temple." Profanity is the use of terms of a serious religious nature in an irreverent, sacrilegious way. To take the name of God in vain or to use sacred religious terms in a blasphemous manner is simply wrong, at all times and in all places. Avoid vulgarity because you are a cultivated person who cares about the sensitivities of others. Avoid profanity because you are a devout person who fears God and honors the worship of God.

Avoid triteness. Trite expressions are ones which have become stale as a result of overuse. Use of such expressions may make your speech or writing appear boring or lacking in creativity. Avoid such clichés as "after all has been said and done," "busy as a bee," "few and far between," "goes without saying," "slow as molasses," "to make a long story short," etc.

Rhetorical Devices

Rhetoric is the art of effective speaking or writing. You can make your speaking or writing more effective by using figurative language, language employing various rhetorical devices. These can be grouped into two types: schemes and tropes. A scheme is an unusual arrangement or ordering of words. A trope is an unusual use of words. Study these common rhetorical devices.

Schemes–unusual arrangements of words

alliteration–repetition of initial letters or sounds

> The summer soldier and the sunshine patriot will, in this crisis,
> shrink from the service of their country. –Thomas Paine

anaphora–repetition of words or phrases

> In time the strong and stately turrets fall,
> In time the rose and silver lilies die,
> In time the monarchs captive are, and thrall,
> In time the sea and rivers are made dry.
> –Giles Fletcher

anastrophe–inversion of the normal order of words

> With this ring I thee wed.
> –The Rite for Matrimony, The Book of Common Prayer

asyndeton–the omission of conjunctions between items in a series

I came, I saw, I conquered. –Julius Caesar

chiasmus–a form of parallelism in which the main parts of the second parallel element are inverted

The sabbath was made for man, and not man for the sabbath. –Mark 2:27

climax–arranging words, phrases, clauses, or whole sentences so that they proceed from the least forceful to the most forceful.

As Caesar lov'd me, I weep for him; as he was fortunate, I rejoice at it; as he was valiant, I honor him; but, as he was ambitious, I slew him.
--William Shakespeare, *Julius Caesar*

ellipsis–omission of words or phrases

What is man,
If his chief good and market of his time
Be but to sleep and feed? a beast, no more. --William Shakespeare, *Hamlet*

parallelism–the repetition of similar grammatical forms

Not by might, nor by power, but by my spirit, saith the Lord of hosts.
–Zechariah 4:6

polysyndeton–the opposite of asyndeton; the use of conjunctions between all the items of a series

Be fruitful, and multiply, and replenish the earth. –Genesis 9:1

Tropes–unusual uses of words

apostrophe–addressing an absent or imaginary person

O death, where is thy sting? O grave, where is thy victory?
–1 Corinthians 15:55

hyperbole–exaggeration

Why, man, he doth bestride the narrow world like a Colossus. . . .
--William Shakespeare, *Julius Caesar*

irony–using words to express the opposite of their literal meaning

> For Brutus is an honorable man;
> So are they all, all honorable men. –William Shakespeare, *Julius Caesar*

litotes–affirming something by negating its opposite

> But Paul said, I am a man which am a Jew of Tarsus, a city in Cilicia, a citizen of no mean city. –Acts 21:39

metaphor–a comparison which suggests a similarity, without using the words *like* or *as*

> The Lord is my shepherd; I shall not want. –Psalm 23:1

metonymy–using the name of one thing for another thing with which it is associated

> What has Athens to do with Jerusalem? –Tertullian

onomatopoeia–the use of words that imitate the sound of the thing named

> They heard the babble of the brook and the splash of the fish.

oxymoron–the joining together of words that seem incompatible

> darkness visible –John Milton

paradox–a statement that seems contradictory to common sense yet which is nonetheless true

> He that findeth his life shall lose it, and he that loseth his life for My sake shall find it. –Matthew 10:39

personification–attributing human qualities or abilities to objects or abstract ideas

> The mountains and the hills shall break forth before you into singing, and all the trees of the field shall clap their hands. –Isaiah 55:12

rhetorical question–A question not intended to elicit an actual answer, but asked with the assumption that only one answer is possible

> Hath not a Jew eyes? hath not a Jew hands, organs, dimensions, senses, affections, passions? ... If you prick us, do we not bleed? If you tickle us, do we not laugh? If you poison us, do we not die? And if you wrong us, shall we not revenge? –William Shakespeare, *The Merchant of Venice*

simile–a comparison using the words *like* or *as*

> Thou shalt be like a watered garden, and like a spring of water, whose waters fail not. –Isaiah 58:11

synecdoche–a type of metonymy in which a part is used to represent a whole

> Give us this day our daily bread. –Matthew 6:11

zeugma–the use of a word in two different ways at the same time

> She left in high spirits and a Cadillac.
> *–American Heritage Dictionary of the English Language*

Glossary of Diction

Take note of these common errors in word usage.

1. accept, except *Accept* is a verb meaning "to receive." *Except* is usually a preposition, meaning "excluding."

> Did you *accept* their invitation to dinner?
> Everyone was there *except* Luke.

2. ad, ed, exam, lab, math, phone, etc. Avoid such abbreviated forms in formal writing. Rather, use the complete word: *advertisement, education, examination, laboratory, mathematics, telephone,* etc.

> This biology course requires that students spend two hours in the *lab* each week. (incorrect)
> This biology course requires that students spend two hours in the *laboratory* each week. (correct)

3. adverse, averse *Adverse* means "unfavorable, harmful." *Averse* means "opposed to."

> Did you have an *adverse* reaction to the medication?
> I am certainly *averse* to such an unconstitutional concentration of power in the federal government.

4. affect, effect *Affect* is always a verb and means "to influence." *Effect* is usually a noun and means "the result of some action." *Effect* can be used as a verb, but when it is it means "to bring about, to produce."

> How will the use of these chemicals *affect* the wider environment?
> One can easily see the *effects* of industrialized agriculture.
> If you wish to *effect* a change, you will have to bolster the diversified family farm.

5. ain't Though used by some in colloquial speech, it is considered inappropriate for standard formal speaking or writing.

> He is the owner, *ain't* he? (incorrect)
> *Isn't* he the owner? (correct)

6. allusion, illusion An allusion is a reference to something. An illusion is an image or belief that is false or imaginary.

> In his speeches Churchill frequently made *allusions* to the Bible and Shakespeare.
> It is an *illusion* to think that we can produce a utopia here on earth.

7. alright, all right The word is correctly written as two words *all right*.

> Is it *alright* with you if I borrow your ladder? (incorrect)
> Is it *all right* with you if I borrow your ladder? (correct)

8. a lot, lots Do not use these to mean "many" or "much."

> *A lot* of the road projects had to be cancelled. (incorrect)
> *Many* of the road projects had to be cancelled. (correct)

9. among, between Use *between* when referring to only two items, *among* when referring to three or more.

The pie was divided *between* the two boys.
The cookies were divided *among* all the children in the class.

10. amount, number *Amount* is used for a quantity of something that cannot be counted, *number* for a collection of items that can be counted.

Such a large *amount* of water will overflow the holding pond.
A large *number* of people attended the meeting.

11. amounts up to Omit the preposition *up*.

The cost of the project could *amount up to* several thousand dollars. (incorrect)
The cost of the project could *amount to* several thousand dollars. (correct)

12. anxious, eager *Anxious* means "to be worried, to have anxiety." *Eager*, on the contrary, means "to look forward to with enthusiasm."

Many people become *anxious* before speaking in public.
The children were *eager* to open their presents.

13. anywheres, everywheres, nowheres, somewheres Omit the *s* at the end of these words.

We could not find the water hose *anywheres*. (incorrect)
We could not find the water hose *anywhere*. (correct)

14. as, because Do not use the conjunction *as* when you mean "since" or "because."

As it was raining, we decided to postpone our trip. (incorrect)
Because it was raining, we decided to postpone our trip. (correct)

15. awful, awfully, terrible, terribly Do not use these as intensives meaning "very" or "extremely."

We are *awfully* happy about their engagement. (incorrect)
We are *extremely* happy about their engagement. (correct)

16. bad, badly *Bad* is an adjective, and *badly* is an adverb. Do not use them interchangeably.

I feel very *badly* about what I said. (incorrect)
I feel very *bad* about what I said. (correct)

After his fall, his leg hurt *bad*. (incorrect)
After his fall, his leg hurt *badly*. (correct)

17. being as, being since Do not use these as subordinating conjunctions in the place of *since* or *because*.

Being as the book was overdue, I had to pay a late fine. (incorrect)
Since the book was overdue, I had to pay a late fine. (correct)

18. beside, besides The preposition *beside* means "by the side of," whereas the preposition *besides* means "in addition to."

The old man's sons stood *beside* him at the ceremony.
Besides new tires, our car also needs a good tune-up.

19. better, had better *Better* is not a verb and should not be used in place of *had better*.

I *better* get to work on my research paper. (incorrect)
I *had better* get to work on my research paper. (correct)

20. between you and I Objects of prepositions should be in the objective case, so say "between you and me," not "between you and I."

Between you and I, I am not sure that we can afford it. (incorrect)
Between you and me, I am not sure that we can afford it. (correct)

21. bunch Avoid using this informal term for "a large group"; use a more precise term.

We met *a bunch* of our neighbors at the community supper. (incorrect)
We met *many* of our neighbors at the community supper. (correct)

22. can, may Use *can* to express ability but *may* to express permission.

Can he walk without his crutches?
May I sit with you?

23. center around This is illogical; something centers *at* or centers *in* or centers *on*, but it cannot center *around*.

> His arguments before the court *centered around* the original intent of the framers of the Constitution. (incorrect)
> His arguments before the court *centered on* the original intent of the framers of the Constitution. (correct)

24. cite, site These two words are easily confused. *Cite* is a verb meaning "to quote or refer to formally." *Site* is a noun meaning "the location of something."

> When quoting or even referring to another work, be sure to *cite* that work in a footnote.
> The *site* of the Battle of Bunker Hill is marked with a monument.

25. disinterested, uninterested These are not synonyms. *Uninterested* means "indifferent, without interest," but *disinterested* means "impartial, not biased."

> My brother seemed *uninterested* in what I was saying.
> Sometimes a *disinterested* third party can help settle a disagreement.

26. double subject Double subjects are redundant and should not be used.

> My *parents they* live on a farm in West Florida. (incorrect)
> My *parents* live on a farm in West Florida. (correct)

27. elicit, illicit *Elicit* is a verb meaning "to evoke or call forth." *Illicit* is an adjective meaning "illegal."

> The speaker tried to *elicit* some laughter with his jokes.
> The mayor was accused of accepting *illicit* payments from people wanting municipal contracts.

28. emigrate, immigrate, emigrant, immigrant *Emigrate* (which contains the Latin prefix *e*, meaning "out of") means "to leave out of a country." *Immigrate* (which contains the Latin prefix *in*, meaning "into") means "to go into a country."

> Her ancestors *emigrated* from Ireland during the potato famine of 1848.
> Several Jewish families *immigrated* to Charleston and Savannah during the colonial period.

29. eminent, imminent These are two adjectives with totally different meanings. *Eminent* means "famous, prominent." *Imminent* means "about to happen."

> Several *eminent* scientists wrote the president, raising questions about the long-term feasibility of the project.
> The crowd stood on the tarmac, awaiting the governor's *imminent* arrival.

30. expect, suspect *Expect* means "to await or watch for." It should not be used in place of the verb *suspect* meaning "to suppose or surmise."

> We are *expecting* them at any moment.
> I *suspect* that you are correct.

31. fewer, less *Less* is used for a quantity of something that cannot be counted, *fewer* for a collection of items that can be counted.

> In an attempt to lose weight, I tried to eat foods with *fewer* calories.
> Unfortunately, I lost *less* weight than my physician had wanted me to lose.

32. good, well *Good* is always an adjective. *Well* is usually used as an adverb; it is used as an adjective only to mean "healthy."

> His first novel was quite *good*.
> For a person with such little experience, he writes *well*.
> Nathaniel was not feeling *well*, so he went to his room to lie down.

33. had of, could of, should of, etc. The *of* sometimes used after *had* is unnecessary and should be omitted. The *of* sometimes used after *could, should, would*, etc. should be *have*.

> If he *had of* told me, perhaps I *could of* helped. (incorrect)
> If he *had* told me, perhaps I *could have* helped. (correct)

34. had ought Do not use *had* with *ought*.

> We *had ought* to act on principle rather than on the basis of pragmatism. (incorrect)
> We *ought* to act on principle rather than on the basis of pragmatism. (correct)

35. hopefully, thankfully *Hopefully* means "in a hopeful manner"; *thankfully* means "in a thankful manner." Do not use these to mean "I hope" or "I am thankful."

> *Hopefully*, we shall be able to finish the roof before the rain. (incorrect)
> *I hope* that we shall be able to finish the roof before the rain. (correct)

> *Thankfully*, no one was injured. (incorrect)
> *I am thankful* no one was injured. (correct)

36. imply, infer To imply is to suggest something; to infer is to interpret or to draw a conclusion.

> Dr. Reid *implied* we would be having a quiz on our reading assignment.
> We *inferred* from what Dr. Reid said that we would be having a quiz on our reading.

37. in, into Note that *in* means "within," but *into* implies movement from outside to inside.

> My father walked *in* the room and looked around. (incorrect)
> My father walked *into* the room and looked around. (correct)

38. inside of, outside of Omit the preposition *of*.

> *Inside of* the front cover is the author's signature. (incorrect)
> *Inside* the front cover is the author's signature. (correct)

39. irregardless Since *regardless* is a negative word and so is the prefix *in* (which drops its *n* and doubles the initial consonant of the word it precedes), this is actually a double negative. Do not use it; rather, use *regardless*.

> Do the right thing, *irregardless* of what unprincipled people may think. (incorrect)
> Do the right thing, *regardless* of what unprincipled people may think. (correct)

40. kind of, sort of Do not use these expressions as adverbs to mean "somewhat" or "rather."

His stomach began to feel *kind of* queasy. (incorrect)
His stomach began to feel *rather* queasy. (correct)

41. kind of a, sort of a The *a* is unnecessary and should be omitted.

What *kind of a* bird is that? (incorrect)
What *kind of* bird is that? (correct)

42. learn, teach Whereas *learn* means "to obtain instruction," *teach* means "to give instruction." Students learn, but teachers teach.

Mr. Calbert *taught* me to read critically, looking for logical fallacies. As a result of his instruction, I *learned* to recognize illogic when I see it.

43. like, as, as if *Like* is a preposition and begins a prepositional phrase. Do not use *like* in an adverb clause in the place of *as* or *as if*.

That looks *like* a Baltimore oriole. (correct)

He speaks *like* he knows what he is talking about. (incorrect)
He speaks *as if* he knows what he is talking about. (correct)

Let me repeat it just *like* he said it. (incorrect)
Let me repeat it just *as* he said it. (correct)

44. loose, lose *Loose* is either an adjective meaning "unfastened, unbound" or a verb meaning "to unfasten, to unbind." *Lose* is always a verb meaning "to be unable to find" or "to fail to keep."

The cover of this book is *loose*.
The king commanded them to *loose* the prisoner.
Did you *lose* your keys again?

45. nauseated, nauseous *Nauseated* is an adjective meaning "feeling nausea," but *nauseous* is an adjective meaning "causing nausea." Something horrible or revolting may be nauseous, but the person who sees it is nauseated.

The doctor asked me if I felt *nauseated*.
She turned away in horror from the *nauseous* sight.

46. pretty Do not use it as an adverb to mean "somewhat," "fairly," or "moderately."

> This old car still runs *pretty* well. (incorrect)
> This old car still runs *fairly* well. (correct)

47. real, really Whereas *real* is an adjective, *really* is an adverb. Do not use *real* as an adverb to intensify another adverb.

> We had a *real* enjoyable dinner together. (incorrect)
> We had a *really* enjoyable dinner together. (correct)

48. reason is because *Because* is a subordinating conjunction and is used to start an adverb clause. In a sentence that begins "The reason is ..." what follows is the predicate nominative. It should therefore be a noun clause rather than an adverb clause. Rewrite the sentence either turning the adverb clause into a noun clause (beginning with *that*) or using the adverb clause beginning with *because* correctly.

> The *reason* for the accident *was because* he was driving too fast. (incorrect)
> The *reason* for the accident *was that* he was driving too fast. (correct)
> He had the accident *because* he was driving too fast. (correct)

49. -self, -selves Such words as *myself, yourself, himself, herself, itself, ourselves, yourselves, themselves* can be used correctly two ways. They may be used after a noun or pronoun to emphasize that noun or pronoun; these are called intensive pronouns. Or they may be used as reflexive pronouns, merely to refer to the subject. They may not be used simply in the place of the personal pronouns for no reason.

> She sewed the dress *herself*. (intensive)
> She *herself* sewed the dress. (intensive)
> The child fell down and hurt *himself*. (reflexive)
> Sit with Margie and *myself*. (incorrect)

50. sensual, sensuous *Sensual* means "pertaining to sexual desires, sexy." *Sensuous* simply means "pertaining to the senses."

> The *sensual* suggestion of Potiphar's wife was rejected by young Joseph.
> The wonderful food, the sparkling crystal, the beautiful china, and the starched linen made the meal truly a *sensuous* experience.

51. some, somewhat Do not use *some* as an adverb to mean "somewhat," "fairly," or "moderately."

> I am feeling *some* better now. (incorrect)
> I am feeling *somewhat* better now. (correct)

52. sure, surely *Sure* is an adjective, and *surely* is an adverb. Do not use *sure* to intensify an adjective or adverb.

> We were *sure* unhappy about the outcome of the election. (incorrect)
> We were *surely* unhappy about the outcome of the election. (correct)

53. that, which, who, whom These relative pronouns are not interchangeable. Use *who* and *whom* to refer only to people; use *which* to refer only to things. You may use *that* to refer to either people or things.

> Is he the one *whom* they chose? (a person)
> Is he the one *that* they chose? (a person)

> Is this the one *which* they chose? (a thing)
> Is this the one *that* they chose? (a thing)

54. them, those *Them* should not be used as an adjective or as a demonstrative pronoun; rather, use *those*.

> Do you know anything about *them* flowers? (incorrect)
> Do you know anything about *those* flowers? (correct)
> *Them* are Old China roses. (incorrect)
> *Those* are Old China roses. (correct)

55. this, that, these, those *This* and *that* are singular demonstrative pronouns and should be used to modify singular nouns. *These* and *those* are plural demonstrative pronouns and should be used to modify plural nouns.

> *This type* of paint will hold up better than *those types*.

56. try and The verb *try* is often followed by an infinitive (as in "try to help"). Infinitives start with the word *to*; do not use *and* in place of *to*.

> *Try and be* on time to class. (incorrect)
> *Try to be* on time to class. (correct)

57. want in, want on, want out, want through Do not use such expressions; be more specific.

> The dog scratched at the door and *wanted in*. (incorrect)
> The dog scratched at the door and *wanted to come in*. (correct)

58. way, ways Do not use *ways* for *way* when referring to distance.

> It is *a long ways* to Idaho from here. (incorrect)
> It is *a long way* to Idaho from here. (correct)

59. where ... at , where ... to It is not wrong to end a sentence in a preposition if that preposition has an object expressed earlier in the sentence (as in "Whom did you give the package to?"). But *where* and *when* are not objects of prepositions; thus, the prepositions *at* and *to* are unnecessary in such expressions. Do not end a sentence in a superfluous preposition.

> *Where* are they living *at*? (incorrect)
> *Where* are they living? (correct)

60. when, where These words are either interrogative words (used to ask a question) or subordinating conjunctions (used to begin adverb clauses). Do not use them to start definitions (which are nouns).

> Hyperbole is *when* you exaggerate for the purpose of emphasis. (incorrect)
> Hyperbole is exaggeration for the purpose of emphasis. (correct)

61. -wise Do not use this suffix to turn a noun into an adverb. Such jargon is very awkward.

> How are we doing *money-wise*? (incorrect)
> How are we doing *financially*? (correct)

62. without, unless *Without* is a preposition and begins a prepositional phrase. *Unless* is a subordinating conjunction and is used to begin an adverb clause.

> *Without* you have your book with you, you cannot follow our discussion of the poems. (incorrect)
> *Unless* you have your book with you, you cannot follow our discussion of the poems. (correct)

Index

CPSIA information can be obtained at www.ICGtesting.com
Printed in the USA
LVOW130337191012

303186LV00011B/1/P